FINDING ME *in the Midst of* CHRONIC PAIN

–

My Story of Healing

VANETTA CALL SERVOSS

Cover Photo by Nastva Kyokka on Unsplash

First paperback edition June 2019

ISBN 978-1-0936-6880-3 (paperback)

Dedication

To my family.
To Brian, BreAnne, KaeLeigh, and JaNelle, whose lives have been changed in ways we never could have imagined or prepared for. Who have stood by me and been some of my greatest cheerleaders.

To those who were there.
To the angels and friends who watched over and cared for me and my family when I couldn't.

To all who have held space for me on this journey.
To those who have nudged and pushed and encouraged and questioned. To John and Michael and Rob and Claire and Dawnne and Carl.

Contents

Foreword

"Stubborn." That's quite possibly Vanetta's favorite word to describe herself. Certainly it's the word that stands out most in my mind as I've observed and conversed with her over these past few years. Usually, as she uttered the word "stubborn," she did so with some amount of something—disdain, perhaps?—for herself. Gradually, though, more bemusement and fondness crept into the word.

Vanetta was learning that what she had thought was a problem and an inherent weakness was actually one of her strongest and best qualities.

I've been privileged to watch as Vanetta has stubbornly dug into and unearthed and examined everything that has kept her stuck in pain, from scar tissue to mistaken interpretations of life experiences and the resulting beliefs, tensions, and pain they led to. It has been a difficult and trying journey, and her stubbornness kept her going one step at a time. It is my belief that we all have such strength inside us, but the trouble is that too many of us are using that stubbornness against ourselves.

In the pages that follow, Vanetta beautifully describes what it took for her to find—and, more importantly—recognize her strength for what it is as she learned how hard she'd been fighting herself. In finding her strength, Vanetta has won her way free of incredible, debilitating, chronic pain.

Her journey is relevant to each of us, because when it comes to the pain each of us is stuck in, we don't differ greatly—rather, it's a matter of the details and degrees of our individual pain. We *all* must walk our own path out of pain. If you would walk out of yours, then you would do well to find, understand, and accept your own stubbornness. This will be your most important journey.

~ Michael Sudbury
Founder of Release Works Myofascial Therapy Clinic

Introduction

I used to think that physical injuries, illnesses, ailments, and difficulties could be resolved by good medical attention and perhaps medication, rest, diet, and exercise...and, if necessary, surgery. I didn't give much thought to how my body worked outside of my basic understanding of anatomy and physiology and general health principles. I thought I had a good understanding of all of those things. I was young. I exercised regularly, tried to eat reasonably well, and considered myself to generally be in good health.

It was a shock to wake up one day and realize that my body was breaking down and that Western medicine could do little to help me. It was a shock to realize that my own understanding of my body could not help me. And even more of a shock to be told I just might have to live with constant pain and limited abilities for the rest of my life.

Lucky for me, I am stubborn.

Lucky for me, I was guided to a way to address and heal my body.

This is my story of healing and the lessons I needed to learn in order to recover from chronic pain. My experience has not at all been what I thought it would be, and yet it has been more than I ever could have hoped for. Not linear, not logical, not straightforward in any way; it has been a twisting, turning, convoluted dive into an exploration of my self, my beliefs, my holding patterns, and my approach to the world. It has been a journey into feeling. And somewhere in the process of all of that, my body, mind, and spirit healed.

My story is unique to me, but I believe many of the lessons I've learned from my journey are universal. Whatever your path, my hope is that you find something here that encourages you and inspires you to keep going.

Part 1: *My World Comes Crashing Down*

1

The Headache from Hell

That Saturday in October started like any other...but quickly became the day I now remember as the day my life changed forever.

For as long as I can remember, I have loved Saturdays. They are the day at the end of the week when I get to sleep in. The day that is slow and lazy and marks the end of a job well done. And if I have done the week right, it is a day when I get to pretty much do whatever I want. The laundry will be washed and folded and maybe even put away. The grocery shopping and errands will be finished. I will get a mommy day off! It's the day with no alarm clocks and no work and no school, the day the kids wake up and get their own cereal for breakfast and watch cartoons, the day their dad takes them to the park to play and I can enjoy some quiet time. The day when I often putter around the house alone.

But not that Saturday.

That Saturday, I woke up with a headache. And that was just not normal. I sometimes woke up with headaches, sure, but rarely (if ever) on a Saturday. And this wasn't just any headache! This was a headache unlike any I had ever experienced before or since. (With the exception, of course, of the months and months and months and more months I had this one...) "Deep, stabbing, throbbing pain" doesn't begin to describe what I felt. I've had plenty of headaches in my lifetime, and I generally categorize them in a few ways. There is the "I didn't get enough sleep and I am really tired right now" headache. The "I have seasonal allergies and I'm miserable" headache. The "I'm dehydrated and need to drink more water or eat something" headache. The "I'm getting sick" headache. And the "I've been around too much noise for too long" headache.

This was none of those.

This one is what I have come to think of as "the headache from hell." It wasn't a migraine—it was pure pain shooting through my skull every time I moved.

Once upon a lifetime ago, I had studied to become a nurse. On top of that, my mom was a nurse practitioner and I had spent time with my three children in the offices of various medical professionals. I had a pretty good idea of how things would go if I sought medical attention. I knew this headache wasn't normal. I also knew that it was a Saturday and that my family doctor's office was not open. And even if it had been and I had bothered to go in, she would most likely have told me to take some Tylenol and come back if things didn't improve.

I skipped the doctor's office and called my mom and took Tylenol. Then I spent the next ten days tracking how my body responded to that and other things. If I was going to go to the trouble to see a doctor for a headache, I was only going to do so after having done everything I could to take care of it myself first.

Here's what I found out.

Ibuprofen didn't touch this headache—this headache laughed at ibuprofen. And acetaminophen. And ibuprofen and acetaminophen stacked on top of each other. It laughed at Advil and it laughed at Advil chased by Mountain Dew. (I can barely make myself drink Mountain Dew, but I tried it because I had read somewhere that caffeine could help pain medication work faster.) This headache didn't blink at any over-the-counter pain relievers. It didn't improve with sleep or rest or decreased stress, not that I thought I had a lot of stress to begin with. It didn't improve with quiet or more water or less junk food. It wasn't allergies and it wasn't sickness and it wasn't going away.

But it did change: it got worse.

It got more intense. It became constant. I woke up with it and went to bed with it. I started to get dizzy. And it wasn't just the base of my skull that throbbed anymore—it was my entire head, especially the right side. This was the type of headache where it hurt to even think: I had trouble pinning down thoughts, and it was difficult to remember things and find words for things. It was difficult to keep my eyes open. Even my brain hurt.

Ten days after the morning I woke up with the headache from hell, I called my doctor's office to make an appointment.

2

Looking For Help

Like many people, I thought seeing a doctor would fix things. The doctor would diagnose what was wrong and tell me what I needed to do, I thought, and I would do what I was told, and things would get better. At the time, I had a great family doctor. I don't know if she appreciated that I had waited ten days before calling her office, but she couldn't argue that I definitely had a not-normal headache. She took some X-rays and diagnosed tension headaches and a straightened cervical spine. She prescribed some muscle relaxants to help with the tension in my neck, a steroid to help the headache, and prescription painkillers to take care of anything that was left. At least, that was my understanding.

I needed stronger medication than I had access to without seeing a doctor. And I did actually have a problem with the alignment of the vertebrae in my neck—that may have been the cause of the tension I was experiencing or the result of it. Either way, the muscle relaxant would take care of it.

At least, that's what I thought.

October 31, 2013

"For all of the wonderful people in our lives who are concerned about me, I have news! Apparently, there has been some tension or stress or something unresolved for a long enough

period of time that the muscles in my neck have tensed and pulled my cervical vertebrae out of a C-curve and into an almost straight line. Translation: I've had a major headache! Just for the record, I had a great time on Saturday, and none of my marvelous and wacky travel companions had anything to do with my current woes. This has been building for a while. Muscle relaxers for several days should solve the problem."

I laugh now at how naïve I was then.

The muscle relaxants didn't help. Neither did the steroids or the prescription painkillers—ten days later, I still had a headache. And I was dizzy more often. I could feel my jaw tighten and tense when I talked. I was feeling pain and tension down into my shoulders, and it was even harder to concentrate than it had been before. I wasn't sleeping well.

The only reason I waited ten days this time to call the doctor was because that was how long the muscle relaxant prescription lasted.

The nurse who checked me in for the second doctor's visit commented that I looked like I didn't feel well. The doctor remarked that I wasn't any better, was I?

I didn't disagree with either of them.

This time, the doctor ordered physical therapy and scheduled me for an MRI of my head and neck. She also referred me to a neurologist and gave me a prescription for a stronger muscle relaxant and painkiller. We agreed that I would see her again to follow up after the MRI and neurology visit.

My Life Changes

By now, my days and weeks were no longer my own.

I started to have to ask for help.

Up to this point in my life, I had considered myself to be an active, capable, fairly healthy mom of three. I was now 38, and I had many responsibilities: homeschooling my children, teaching an early-morning youth class, and giving piano lessons in the afternoons. I was involved in church groups, homeschool groups, and the local YMCA. I loved walking and running and gardening. I was the chief meal preparer, bread baker, party planner, and housekeeper. People counted on me for things. Life was busy and full. I did not have time for this headache.

That all changed overnight.

My life had come to a screeching, crashing halt.

> *November 18, 2013*
>
> *"I woke up this morning with the last of my responsibilities essentially removed. I was told yesterday that I cannot return to teaching in the mornings; the process to replace me as the teacher has begun. I know that it is not medically advisable that I continue to do much of anything until my health matters are resolved. However, aside from the love and concern I have for the youth, teaching was the last thing I had left that helped me feel that I am able to do anything that is worthwhile or good right now. Everything else that generally gives me a sense of identity, purpose, or accomplishment—or even enjoyment—has gradually been stripped away over the past several weeks. I've started to think about all of the things I currently cannot do without eventually (if not immediately) winding up with headaches, dizziness, or muscle tension. And I have realized a few things.*
>
> *There are so many things that create our identity and our sense of purpose and accomplishment each day. For me, most*

if not all of these have been removed, placed on hold, or are not currently possible. I have been left with the very basic core of who I am. My role as a mother generally involved cooking—which I enjoy—baking, keeping the house in order, running errands, shopping, etc. I have not done those things for many weeks now, and what little I do causes headaches and muscle tension. My role as a wife is to support Brian, give hugs, provide encouragement, and take care of his home and children. Now all I can do is hold his hand and give him really pathetic hugs.

The two things that cause the most muscle tension and the worst headaches are sitting for prolonged periods of time and playing the piano. Sitting with my family at dinner becomes uncomfortable. Typing and using the computer have to be done sparingly, as they cause muscle tension that leads to headaches. I love music, and playing the piano is something I have always done to relieve stress and calm my spirit and just for enjoyment. Playing the organ and reading the words of the hymns is soothing and helps me feel close to the spirit. All of these activities are now physically difficult, with painful consequences for my head and neck. Reading is something I enjoy doing, yet holding a book at eye level for any length of time is uncomfortable (even if I don't have a headache). Placing a book in my lap and leaning my head forward to read is pretty much impossible.

I love food, yet I lost my appetite weeks ago. To eat requires significant effort and often pulls at the muscles across my head or causes my jaw to hurt. I find no pleasure in food; generally, eating is not worth the effort. Talking or visiting causes muscle tension; I cannot make eye contact frequently with whomever I'm visiting because doing so causes muscle tension, and if I talk for any length of time, my jaw muscles start to tense and my tongue feels slow. Sometimes even listening causes sounds to reverberate across the muscles and bones of my skull and causes discomfort.

I am not complaining, but as I thought about the removal of my role as a seminary teacher, I realized it was one of the last things I had left that had brought me a sense of purpose, accomplishment, and enjoyment. I'm not sure who I am right now without all of that."

November 21, 2013

"I have gotten used to the fact that I pretty much can't move without hurting, and I have accepted that when I do move, it is going to be slowly. I can handle not eating much because I am not hungry anyway. A bit of insomnia last week was kind of new and interesting because I have never felt wide awake all the time, day and night, for seven days in a row. But to be so very, very tired and not able to sleep might be the thing that finally gets me. . ."

I started to have to cancel things: the piano recital in the fall that my students had been preparing for, the piano lessons I had been giving them to help them prepare, the early-morning youth classes I couldn't find substitutes for. Homeschool lessons and outings. Family activities. Life.

It became impossible to hide how bad things were getting.

I wasn't walking, much less running or going to the gym. In fact, I was barely getting out of bed in the morning. People started to pick up my children in the morning and keep them until my husband picked them up in the evenings after work. Dinners someone else had made frequently showed up on our table. Homeschool was about survival...for all of us. I don't really know what my children studied that fall.

I wasn't sleeping. I wasn't eating. I was barely moving. It hurt to lay down. It hurt to stand up. It hurt to move. It hurt to breathe. The motion and effort it took to talk for any length of time or to chew and swallow food made my jaw lock up. When I sat, it felt like a piece of rebar was being shoved into my brain; when I tried to lay down, I thought my head was going to explode. I took up residence on the couch downstairs, semi-reclining, somewhat drugged on painkillers, dizzy, hurting, and just watching the hours tick by. I couldn't remember the last time I had slept for any length of time. When I did try to sleep, I would frequently be awakened by pain. I lost track of days at a time.

I couldn't remember the last time I didn't hurt.

The dizziness was so bad that I often didn't trust myself to drive. I loved my manual-transmission Honda Civic, but I didn't have the strength to kick in the clutch and shift, much less drive safely considering how many medications were in my body. It hurt to get in and out of our van. Neighbors and friends took turns driving me to physical therapy. I remember sitting in the office before my appointments, trying to find a way to perch on the edge of the chair and position myself so that I wouldn't hurt when I took a breath. It wasn't possible—sitting was just awful. I tried not to breathe.

The physical therapist did his best to realign my cervical spine. It was painful, though. The sessions were fairly short and included teaching me how to do exercises that would (supposedly) strengthen the muscles in my neck and back. I was asked to do three sets of 12 chin tucks and three sets of 12 shoulder retractions. I was told the muscles in my back and shoulders and at the back of my neck were weak. I don't know about "weak"—"tightened and immovable steel cords" felt more accurate.

I quickly found out that the prescribed exercises made me hurt worse: the first set of chin tucks intensified the headache, and the second set felt like it locked up my neck. I couldn't do a third set. Same with the shoulder retractions—it was just too painful. My muscles would spasm.

I discussed these problems with my physical therapist, and we agreed that maybe I should hold off on doing those exercises. I continued working with him for about eight more visits, until he had done all he could to realign my neck.

Nothing changed—I kept having the headaches, muscle tension, and dizziness. He knew I was in a great deal of pain when he discharged me but was unable to do anything to address it.

I had an MRI and found out afterward when I read the report that my doctor was looking for a brain tumor or an aneurysm. Fortunately, neither was found. Also fortunately, I didn't know that was what they were looking for. I had no idea that severe headaches of unknown origin (which was exactly what I was experiencing) were reason to suspect a brain tumor or aneurysm. I'm glad I didn't know! My family and I were already worried enough about my health issues without adding that concern on top of everything else.

It took a month to get in to see a neurologist, but that was mostly a formality. The MRI had showed that I had two small disc protrusions in my neck, but as far as the neurologist could tell, those weren't the cause of my problems. For $350 and ten minutes of his time, he told me there was nothing he could do to help...and sent me back to my family doctor.

A month later, I was back in her office, worse off than the last time she had seen me.

Another prescription for painkillers and muscle relaxants. Talk of ordering a spinal tap to rule out meningitis. Talk of consulting with a chiropractor. See her again in a month. Try wearing a neck brace to allow the muscles in my neck to rest.

Rinse. Cycle. Repeat.

And...I'm back again a month later. No better. Getting tighter and tighter.

By then, Thanksgiving had come and gone. We only had Thanksgiving that year because dear friends invited us to join them. I don't remember much about Christmas except that my family and I wondered if it was the last one we would spend together.

In between visits to my family doctor to renew prescriptions and discuss other options, getting an MRI, and waiting to see the neurologist, I also tried everything else I could think of on my own.

One friend loaned me her TENS unit. I don't know what a TENS unit is supposed to do, but I know that the stimulation from this one turned my neck and shoulders into a solid block of tension—imagine steel cables electrified and tightened by a factor of ten.

Another friend highly recommended I see his acupuncturist. The therapist was kind and knowledgeable, and I tried three visits. The first one didn't help, but it also didn't hurt. The second visit was uncomfortable and two of the needles had to be repositioned in order to hurt less. The third visit was downright painful and all of the needles hurt despite some of them being repositioned. The acupuncturist did not recommend that I continue seeing him.

Someone else drove me back and forth to see a massage therapist for a few visits, but it hurt to be touched and it hurt to be massaged. My shoulder blades were glued to my ribs. My neck was a mess. My body was clenched tight. I hoped, though, that if the tightness and tension could be relieved, then the pain would also ease. I gritted my teeth through most of my time with the massage therapist and wound up hurting worse afterward.

I tried SalonPas topical patches, heat packs, and ice packs. I felt minty, overheated, and cold in turn...but not better.

I visited a chiropractor who recommended that I never have my neck adjusted due to an incompletely closed dens in my cervical vertebrae. I researched potentially helpful diets, but I didn't find anything worth pursuing. I even considered dry needling, but I was too chicken to try it.

At best, nothing helped. Most things actually made the pain and muscle tension worse. It wasn't just a headache anymore—I felt like my body was slowly locking up. Sounds would vibrate and pound through my head, and even my own voice felt loud inside. It hurt to be touched. And nobody knew why, much less how to help.

Things You Never Want to Hear Your Doctor Say

After four months of multiple rounds of painkillers, muscle relaxants, doctor and therapist visits, bedrest, and worry, I was worse off than I was when I started.

And I was back in my family doctor's office. I will never forget that day, either.

She looked at me after we talked about how I was doing. And then she said words that would send my life in another new direction: she acknowledged that we had done all that she knew to try, and she said, "I don't know what else to tell you. Maybe you should try myofascial release."

I am forever grateful for her honesty.

I didn't know what myofascial release was. I didn't care. I honestly don't believe she thought it would change anything, but I was beyond desperate at this point.

It took three weeks to get into the physical therapy office that could help me.

Looking back, I wish it could have been sooner. At the time I was grateful to have one more option before giving up completely.

3

What I Had Ignored and Why That Mattered

I'm going to interject here a bit about what I have learned since my family doctor said those words to me that day. People have often asked why things happened the way they did. Did I have an accident or surgery that caused it? Was it an illness? Why did that happen to me?

In those early weeks and months, I kept asking myself, "Why?!"

Over time, I have gradually become able to somewhat answer that question.

I've learned that it wasn't just about the headache—that was simply the thing that finally got my attention. Looking back, I can see that my body had been slowly falling apart and needing help for years. I just hadn't paid attention. Didn't know I needed to. Didn't know it mattered. Wouldn't have known what to do about it even if I *had* been paying attention. I had to literally be stopped in my tracks in order to learn what my body needed. The headache was the straw that broke the camel's back.

But there were plenty of straws before that.

Early in my college years, I discovered running. That eventually led to crippling pain in my shins. And you know that creaking sound the shins can make and the popping sound knees can make? That's crepitus, and I had that. It made it difficult to walk for many weeks. But I kept trying to run the hills of Rexburg, Idaho anyway...until it became painfully clear that I couldn't.

In my 20s, I had an unanticipated C-section. I had strong feelings about the pregnancy and the ensuing surgery but couldn't admit that to anyone. Scar tissue started to spread and wrap inside around my bladder, sacrum, and pelvic bones. I started to brace and clench in my lower back when I would bend over or lift anything. At the time, the C-section was just an unplanned and unexpected surgery, one that I wasn't aware I would need. But aware of it or not, the internal landscape of my body was changing.

Again in my 20s, another C-section. Again a pregnancy and surgery accompanied by more strong feelings that I couldn't admit to having. (One might think I would have learned something the first time...) I remember the first time I felt my back go out after that second surgery—I was squatting to return a volleyball, and I felt something give. Wasn't able to stand back up. Shooting pain and weakness froze me in that partial squat as I was introduced to lower back problems for the first time in my life. For the first time, I was aware there might be something going on in my back that I should consider being concerned about.

Fast-forward to a root canal that made me feel physically ill from the pain of it. It felt like someone was digging in my brain. I felt such intense stabbing pain through my eye and temple that it made me nauseous, a feeling that lingered for a long time afterward. That pain still resurfaces occasionally with intra-oral myofascial work.

A job in a cafeteria led to a repetitive stress injury in my wrists and spending a few weeks with a brace on one hand and making only cautious movements with the other. I was able to keep working and compensate by moving a bit slower. Playing the organ or piano was an interesting challenge for a while. I just worked through that pain because there were things that needed doing.

At age 32, I spent a year dealing with recurring strep throat. I was on and off antibiotics for months...in and out of the doctor's office like clockwork every 30 days because my body couldn't seem to get rid of the infection. I was eventually referred to an infectious disease specialist and told I had contracted Epstein-Barr virus at some point and would always be susceptible to that. After months of unsuccessful antibiotics, finally had my tonsils removed. Worst 11 days of recovery in my life! I do *not* recommend anyone have their tonsils removed as an adult. More scar tissue formed as a result.

I spent years engaging in high-impact, high-stress daily exercise, pushing my body past where it probably should have been pushed many, many times. I did 1 ½ to two hours of exercise a day, often five days a week, and I was proud of it because I was finally losing weight. Kept ignoring the constant tightness and muscle aches; kept believing the tiredness was normal given the intensity of my workouts. Believed the aches and pains and stiffness I felt when moving or standing or getting up and down out of a chair or into and out of a car was also normal.

In my mid-30s, I trained for and completed three half-marathons, spending hours and hours running. I loved that time with my friends! But I ended up wearing a brace on my foot for much of the time I spent training for the last half-marathon. The crepitus in my shins was back, and so was my ankle weakness and heel pain. Sometimes, I limped; often, I had to compensate. It was difficult to walk without constant pain. Still, I was determined to run that last race. Walked much of the second half... Encouraged my friends to go on without me because I was not completely sure I was going to finish. I was too stubborn to *not* finish, but I didn't want to slow my friends down while I limped through the remainder of the course.

Somewhere in the midst of all that, I started and completed a Master's program...in health promotion, of all things! (Again, you might think I would be learning something...) Somehow managed to fit my studies into a carefully structured life of homeschooling and exercising and teaching and sleeping. I was doing it all! Convinced I had no stress as long as nobody messed with my schedule. I kept pushing through the tiredness and frequent headaches, kept trying to eat right and get enough sleep and enough exercise and enough time with my family. Yep, no stress at all.

Eventually, I became a group fitness instructor at the YMCA, in the process swapping my personal exercise routine for a group setting. Pushing myself even harder now that I was the one in front of the class, always stressing about my appearance and keeping my weight down. Sometimes I taught two or three classes a day. I was a wet, sweaty, tired mess. Still trying to do it all, but tired, so tired. Always sore. And starting to get injured, too—tweaked my knee during step aerobics class, tweaked it again during spin class. My ankle sometimes felt like it was collapsing, and I was constantly monitoring and protecting my back. (And of course I also had aftereffects of the bumps and bruises and falls I most certainly had as a child.) But I never slowed down! I'd go home and nap after classes.

By the time pain stopped me in my tracks, I had accumulated years of unaddressed stress and tension and injuries. Scar tissue from surgeries had been twisting and tightening and wrapping around things for years without being addressed. Aches and pains had been compensated for instead of being addressed. Fatigue had become the norm.

It is ludicrous to think I just had a headache!

As I mentioned in the introduction, my Master's degree in health promotion was woefully inadequate in helping me understand health in a way that could actually help me when things got bad. It was painfully clear that my health was *not* just about diet and exercise and disease prevention. I had studied anatomy and physiology, behavioral health, nutrition, and human growth and development. I had taught others about behavior modification and changing habits and balancing life to optimize health. Nothing had prepared me for the possibility that my understanding of my body was incomplete. Or that I might one day run up against a physical challenge that couldn't be fixed by medical science or exercising more or changing my dietary habits.

I woke up recently one morning and realized how lucky I am that my life fell apart when it did. Instead of spending the next 50 years living the way I had been living and suffering the way I had been suffering, somehow I was lucky enough to be shut down completely and shown a different way.

In hindsight, I can see how lucky I was.

At the time, not so much.

Part 2: Putting the Pieces Back Together

4

It Becomes Apparent This is Not Going to be a Quick Fix

I'm not going to lie: this has not been an easy journey. It wasn't just a matter of going to a new therapist for a new therapy for a few weeks or a few months or even a year and being "fixed." If that was what had happened, this would be a really short and boring story.

For me, myofascial release has been a major and necessary component in healing. I often consider it **the** component of healing. But it hasn't been something that was done *to* me that somehow made me better—it is a process that has required consistent and frequent treatments and my active involvement and presence. And that has been difficult. I have found that I am a slow (although thorough) learner and often require multiple repetitions of a message in order to fully integrate understanding and change.

As I slowly grasped the fact that regaining function in my body was not going to happen quickly, I had to shift my thinking and expectations and start to notice indicators of progress. Some were larger than others, but many were very small, and it often felt like I was taking two steps forward and one step back. Sometimes it even felt like a half-step forward and three steps back. But there was progress! There were also some major potholes and occasional bottomless pits that I would fall into.

This has been a gut-wrenching, not-for-the-faint-of-heart, sometimes-(often)-want-to-quit journey. A journey I never intended to go on in the first place.

But one that has been worth every bit of effort.

I'm Introduced to Myofascial Release Therapy

I believe there are numerous pivot points in everyone's life, points where the direction someone is headed in can drastically change. February 28, 2014 was one of those pivot points for me. That was the day I walked into the physical therapy office where I met John Petrides and I was introduced to the modality I credit with saving my life. At the time of this writing, almost five years later, I am still regularly seeing a John-Barnes-trained myofascial release therapist.

Some might be wondering, "Could myofascial release *really* have saved her life? And if she's healed, why is she still seeing a therapist?"

I'm glad you asked.

What I have found since I got sick is that my idea of health and wellness and healing was incomplete. None of the education I had received had ever mentioned the role of the fascial system in maintaining or recovering health. Never mentioned the role of emotions in bracing or clenching. Never mentioned the importance of the relationship between the mind and the body.

My journey to healing has required that I examine a lot of things in my life and in my beliefs that I didn't even know were there. A lot that I didn't want to believe were there. A lot of "things" that I hoped would never *be* "things."

During my first visit, I was scared. The shut down, clenched tight, braced, hurting, confused, highly uncomfortable, easily embarrassed, flushing or breaking out into a rash when asked a direct question, kind of scared. I don't know what I was expecting when I first met John Petrides and was introduced to myofascial release, but I do know I was *not* expecting a dimly lit room, a massage table, and almost two hours of discussion, evaluation, hands-on manual therapy, and questions I didn't know how to answer.

But that's how it began. We decided I did indeed need help and set up an initial schedule of two visits per week for the next ten weeks.

Each session after that initial one would start with a quick assessment of my posture. Oh, how I hated that! I would stick my hands deep into my pockets (if I had them) and then try to hold still. John would quietly ask me to let my hands hang by my side. And could I please stop shifting? I did my best, but I hated feeling examined and judged. Vulnerable. Exposed. Seen.

I kept going to the appointments anyway. . .

. . .And stayed shut down for many months. Barely talked to him. Couldn't look him in the eye. Often (still) broke out in a rash during the assessment. But kept going.

If I hadn't been desperate, there's no way I ever would have considered that myofascial release might actually help. If I hadn't been desperate, I never would have stuck with it long enough to find out that it actually did.

But I *was* desperate, and I *did* stick with it. And somehow, despite being in my own way, I started to see progress where I had previously only seen a downward spiral.

April 14, 2014

"Six weeks ago, the best I could do for a physical therapy goal was to hope to eventually not hurt all the time. Today, I got a new goal: to be able to run again. I don't know how long it will take to get there, but it sounds like a great goal to me! Although my 'wise' children pointed out that I already am able to run—it just happens to be at the speed of a turtle running through peanut butter..."

April 21, 2014

"Woo-hoo!! I walked a whole mile this morning! And it only took 32 minutes and 49 seconds. Go, turtle, go!"

April 23, 2014

"I guess I won't give up today."

Ten weeks into the appointments, it was clear that healing was going to be a slow process.

"I've read about others who had relief after just a few sessions. Read about how gentle mfr (myofascial release) was. I've wondered what my problem was and if mfr would really help. Going to therapy was really hard. What I now know must have been gentle touch at the time still really hurt—it set off an instant sense of blackness and intense pressure in my head and chest along with increased pain. I would go to therapy and often leave feeling the same or worse. I often went directly home afterward and slept for several hours. I needed the two days in between appointments to recover, and then I would go back and do it again. I did this for six months without seeing any significant progress... It was the little things that gradually accumulated over time that helped me keep trusting the work, that and the knowledge that mfr was my last option.

So I kept going. Six months in, I was still fatigued all the time and couldn't lift things or exert much energy without relapsing into headaches and dizziness. Was walking really slowly and not moving much... But I was moving."

I started to engage with my family more, doing things like roasting hotdogs and marshmallows in the backyard. Slowly, I was beginning to walk a bit—sometimes for a mile, sometimes less, always slowly. But I was walking again. Spring came and went, and I made arrangements for our annual get-together with friends to play kickball on Memorial Day. Not surprisingly, I didn't play...but I *did* make those arrangements. In June, I attended a church girls' camp as a youth leader. And in September, our family chose to move across the country to Idaho. Things were looking up physically.

But that was just the tip of the iceberg.

I was still shut down inside. There was a progress sheet I was asked to fill out at the beginning of every session with my therapist, and I started using it as a way to communicate to him the things I couldn't admit out loud. Started to ask questions about the process of healing. Started to share things I was feeling and struggling with. I would write notes to my therapist, and he would read them while I quietly watched, hoping he wouldn't judge me or ask me anything. And then we would have a treatment session.

Most of my memories of those early months of visits are of gentleness and patience, although occasionally John would ask a question or make a comment that would stop me in my tracks, triggering emotions that would make me shut down inside. Tears finally burst out of me during one of the last visits we had together that year. John commented that those tears had been a long time coming.

I was very aware of how many times I had suppressed emotions during our sessions, biting my tongue, clenching my jaw, bracing tight. Even once covering my head with a pillow so that he wouldn't see the tears I could feel forming.

I remember the time he asked if I was depressed. Had I considered talking to someone? My immediate internal response was "No!!" I could barely talk to John! Why would I ever consider seeing someone in a setting where all I was supposed to *do* was talk?! My external response was to hold very still and become even more quiet.

> *"There were so many, many times when I would leave a session feeling worse than I did when I went in. I would go in with a pain level of 6 or 7 on a 10-point pain scale, and everything my therapist did or touched would just intensify that. A light touch on my sternum felt like an elephant sitting on my chest and was accompanied by feelings similar to a panic attack, making it really difficult to breathe; what must have been really light cranial work was incredibly painful. Headaches and dizziness were the initial reasons I started going to mfr, and cranial work seemed to make those problems worse. There has been a lot of what I can only describe as 'blackness' in my head, and I would brace against it even as I was trying my best to soften. A lot of sessions were really difficult, physically and emotionally.*
>
> *But deep down, I also knew it was important for me to keep going even though I was uncomfortable the whole time, really uncomfortable. Mostly with myself, because I did trust my therapist and could feel his genuine love. Still do. Still can. But that love doesn't make therapy sessions any easier or less painful. Ultimately, all I could do was just take more time and put in a lot more work and learn and grow and find me under all the gunk that was there.*
>
> *Light touch is still fairly painful to those areas that are stuck in something, and I still leave some therapy sessions feeling a whole lot worse than I did going in. I am still uncomfortable a*

lot of the time. And it is still a struggle sometimes to go to sessions when I need to. Many times, I have wondered what part of mfr is 'gentle,' because that is not what I feel when I go. But I can see the changes in myself...I can feel the changes in myself. Experiencing increased pain during therapy has been part of my process, probably an important one because I have had to be really determined in my efforts when things didn't seem to be getting any better and moving forward was really difficult."

I frequently asked, "How much longer do I have to do this?" I was frustrated that things seemed so slow. I didn't understand that it was a journey, a process. I was reading everything I could find about myofascial release in an effort to understand what it was and how it could help, but still not grasping that it was a process. I didn't grasp that it was not a matter of fixing, but rather a matter of healing.

John never did have an answer for how long it would take. But when I asked, he would remind me that when I first started seeing him, I could barely walk down the hall.

That would generally cause me to pause for a moment and consider that yes, I was improving, just not as fast as I would like. And I continued to wonder how long I would need to see a therapist. Twice a week for two months gradually stretched to six months. Those initial 20 visits became 20 more. And then more. Still twice a week.

When would I be done??

I was improving, but so slowly. I did not have the strength or energy to pack our house to move that fall. Many good friends helped do that. It is an interesting thing to move and later unpack when you have no clue where to look for things or how things were packed or how the boxes were labeled...

Even with very little stimulus, my body still tensed and tightened, and I would tire quickly with any exertion. My sister helped my daughters and me drive across the country because I couldn't do it alone even though it was a drive I loved and had regularly made alone with my children many times in previous years.

I didn't know how long I was going to take to heal. But I knew that when we moved from Southaven, Mississippi to Shelley, Idaho, I needed to find another therapist.

A Quick Word About Myofascial Release

It seems important to pause here for just a moment to talk about myofascial release as a therapeutic modality, because when I started to receive treatment, it was important to me to understand as much as I could. Admittedly, for a long time, my understanding was primarily on an intellectual level. That intellectual learning eventually just became a lesson for me in learning to get out of my own way.

I read everything I could find when I first started seeing John Petrides for therapy sessions. I wanted to know what I was getting into! I wanted to understand how it could help and how it worked and why I should believe it would, so I read. I read as many books from my therapist's office as I could borrow and as many other books and blog posts about healing as I could find. *Healing Ancient Wounds* by John Barnes; *A Patient's Guide to Myofascial Release* by Cathy Covell; *Waking the Tiger* by Peter Levine; *The Four Agreements* by Don Miguel Ruiz; *What's In Your Web* by Phil Tavolacci. I watched YouTube videos about the fascial tissue and later became aware of The International Fascial Research Congress. I watched snippets of Fireside Chats with John Barnes and videos of unwinding. I joined Facebook groups and lurked there, following the experiences of others. I bought self-help books and listened to podcasts.

I wrote down pages and pages of questions in my journal and on little sticky notes that I would take to my appointments with John. Some, I asked; many, I didn't.

And I still didn't really understand.

I read that myofascial release used gentle, sustained pressure into areas of restriction. That the fascial tissue is like an uninterrupted three-dimensional web, completely connected from head to toe. And that over time—due to injuries, stress, illness, surgery, repetitive postures, and all the bumps and bruises of life—fascial tissue can dehydrate and glue together. It becomes restricted, and things start to hurt. As a therapist applies carefully timed pressure in areas of restriction, those areas will gradually soften and melt away. Things that have been stuck and glued and painful will become soft and pliable. Tissues will "release," and clients will feel better.

That was my understanding for a long time. And I wondered why for me, sessions seemed to not be working the way I had read they would work—instead of feeling like I was melting and lengthening and opening, I felt tight and stiff and in pain.

But the problem was not my therapist or the modality: the problem was me.

Myofascial release as taught by John Barnes and properly applied and received does all I had read and more. But it cannot be understood completely on an intellectual level, and that was my problem. I was thinking and bracing instead of softening into what I was feeling, mostly because I was trying really hard to understand, not feel. In fact, I was actively trying to not feel what was happening in my body.

Talking and thinking is not feeling.

It didn't matter how much I read or thought I understood. The thing I missed for a long time was the need for my awareness to be in my body and not in my head; I didn't realize I had to be willing to feel. That is what much of my learning has been about: learning to feel. Learning to admit what I feel. Learning to allow and even embrace what I feel.

The fascial tissue of the body is amazing (and that is a vast understatement!) and only beginning to be understood by researchers and scientists, yet John Barnes has been teaching for years that it is the container of our consciousness. That the fascial tissue holds memories and emotions. That it gets stuck on more levels than just the physical. That myofascial release is not about feeling better, but about getting better at feeling.

I have had to get a lot better at feeling in order to heal!

Finding a New Therapist

Sometimes, I am more self-aware than I am at other times; sometimes, there is a deep knowing inside that I have learned to trust and that I do my best to act on.

When our family decided to move across the country, it was apparent that I needed continued help. I knew it was essential to find a new therapist *before* we moved—I needed to set up an appointment that would be waiting for me when we arrived in Idaho. There was a deep knowing inside that if I did not have an appointment waiting for me, I would never make one. Finding a new therapist before we moved was a way to hold myself accountable to continuing to make progress.

The problem was that the nearest therapist to our new home turned out to be four hours away, in Boise. The one in Salt Lake City, Utah was only marginally closer.

I faced a choice: how much did I want to pursue what had been helping? What was it worth to me?

I was beginning to understand what deep knowing was about.

I had seen changes. Not as much as I wanted, but more than I had thought was possible given where I had been earlier in the year. I knew I wanted more.

The question was, did I want it enough to drive 200 miles each way for an appointment? And how often could I realistically do that? This was one of those times when I had to pose the question: if getting help wasn't convenient or reasonable, surely it was okay to wonder if it was really meant to be. Surely if I was meant to get the help I needed, it would be more easily accessible. I struggled with that question, all the while *knowing* that I still needed help. Getting it was going to take effort and desire and determination on my part.

How much did I want it?

I decided I wanted help enough to finally pluck up the courage to send email inquiries to the two therapists I had found in Salt Lake City. I wanted help enough to pick up the phone and talk to one of them when I eventually had questions that couldn't easily be answered by email. I wanted help enough to try out a new therapist when I was on vacation in Utah the month before we moved.

These may not seem like significant things, but remember, after months of seeing the same therapist in Mississippi, I was still barely talking to him. I did not talk about myself easily; I hated admitting I needed help. Having to call someone I had never met and talk to them about problems I was having—and asking for help, too—was something that took me a long time to work up the courage to do. And doing so caused enough inner anxiety for me that the person on the other end of the phone picked up on it.

August 15, 2014 was another one of those pivot points in my life. It was the day I walked into the Myofascial Release of Salt Lake office and met Michael Sudbury for the first time. If possible, I was even more scared and shut down and uncomfortable than I had been the first day I met John. Enough so that Michael commented on it...which only made me more uncomfortable.

It was like starting over.

And I hated the process even more than I did the first time! I quickly found that seeing Michael was nothing like seeing John.

I would drive for over three hours to get to the appointment and then sit in the car and argue with myself about needing to go in and not wanting to. Walking into that office meant being seen—I was absolutely sure that Michael could see right through me, could see all of the insecurities and fears and things I didn't like about myself, things I was trying to hide. I hated that. He would greet me, and I would shut down. Ten seconds after walking into the office, I'd be clenched and braced tight. Anything I had planned to say or had considered sharing would be tightly locked away again. I would beat myself up for not being brave enough to speak up, for being so stubborn, for being so afraid. And I'd be angry that I couldn't admit any of that. Every time I intended to say something, all it took was for Michael to say hi or ask me how I was, and I would shut down.

I hated feeling seen.

I marvel that I made any progress at all.

I'd be clenched and braced tight almost from the moment I walked into the office...actually, from the moment I drove into the parking lot. Frequently, I'd be biting a hole in the inside of my lip throughout the entire session, and I'd leave the session feeling more tight and sore and angry than I was when I arrived.

A word of advice to those who are seeking help: clenching and bracing and trying to hide is counterproductive to the change you are hoping for. It took me years to really learn this.

Still, I just kept showing up. I was too stubborn to give up. And there was still that part of me deep down inside that knew this was something I needed.

> *July 23, 2015*
>
> *"I have felt so many times like I am wasting my time and my therapist's time. And then there's the expense of it all... I have had more than one person ask why I keep going. More than once, I considered quitting. This has been a hard and long process for me. I read as much as I can; I want to believe this will help. Last year, I could see just enough change to keep holding on to that hope. And I kept going.*
>
> *It has been a matter of time and determination and repetition and facing a lot of things I never knew were there.*
>
> *Another six months, and a lot more therapy. (Although I don't go as often now because I moved.) I did a healing seminar, too, and have really started to have days where I feel somewhat better physically. I'm careful with what I do and I see my therapist as often as I can.*
>
> *Six more months, and I continue to feel better. I know my triggers. I do lots and lots of self-care. Some days I feel really really good. Those are rare, but I do have them now. Some days I feel lousy. On those days, I take the time to do what I need to do, whether it is resting or stretching or scheduling an mfr session. I still have baggage."*

And I kept showing up.

July 29, 2015

"I am experiencing the worst healing crisis yet on this mfr journey: excruciating pain in my lower back with even the slightest movement. The pain is paralyzing; it brings me to my knees and stops me in my tracks. I feel absolutely demoralized, humiliated, humbled. Completely dependent on others. Crumpled and beaten into submission.

I give up. I have met something inside that's stronger and uglier and more stubborn than any amount of determination I have left. Beaten by something I cannot understand. That feels as unfair as it is excruciating. I have felt this way before, and I told myself I never wanted to feel this way again. That I was going to do everything I could to never again feel so helpless and dependent and in pain. But I'm feeling it all over again right now: the bracing in a futile attempt to alleviate pain, the helplessness, even the feeling sorry for myself that I refused to feel completely in Monday's therapy session."

And I kept showing up.

September 21, 2015

"Sometimes, I feel like I am living in a bubble that I think is protective but that is mostly restrictive. I stay in that bubble because I think it is safe. The boundary that protects me is made up of the expectations of others—the 'shoulds' and the 'should-nots.' The rules that give order to my life. Boundaries of what is acceptable and what is not. Somebody telling me what to do and think and feel. As long as I follow those rules, there is implied safety. Safety from what? I am not sure. I think I don't want to be afraid. Or hurt. Or feel.

But I have come to realize that the really strong emotions penetrate the bubble's wall and that most of them are painful.

I also realize that I am keeping the wall in place because I am afraid to choose to fully feel. How do I let myself feel when my experience has been that most of what I feel hurts? When letting myself feel in therapy sessions keeps bringing up sadness and anger and loss and anguish? When letting myself feel outside of therapy sessions does the same?

I wonder sometimes why I keep doing this to myself. I know it is because I keep hoping there is something on the other side of all those things. I get glimpses sometimes. But I wonder sometimes if the trade-off is worth it. The restrictive bubble seems awfully attractive when most of what I see outside of it is painful. I am struggling this morning to move toward something that I know I need to move toward. But how do I keep going when there doesn't seem to be an end to the things that hurt?"

Did I mention that this journey is not for the faint of heart?

Life felt like a rollercoaster of ups and downs, sometimes with a lot fewer ups than downs. A gradually-progressing-upward rollercoaster, you could say...although with a lot more downs. The ups were great, though!

Some of the fun progress I started to see was when I could do simple things again, like carry a gallon of milk from the car, up the four steps of the front porch, and into the house without feeling exhausted. Or being able to walk up the 13 steps from the basement to the main floor of the house without having to pause to rest. Never thought things like that would feel like an accomplishment, but at the time, it was huge. After a year of therapy, I could go grocery shopping alone again!

I also made enough progress to be able to scrape the ice off of my own windshield. Again, probably not a big deal to those who haven't struggled, but it took a long time to regain the ability to lift my arms and shoulders so that I could reach out over the windshield. Not something I had ever thought I would be excited to do, but I often still remember that "Woo-hoo! I can scrape my own windshield again!" feeling when I effortlessly do it now. (Side note: I don't actually enjoy scraping my windshield. It is usually really cold outside when I do, and I often complain loudly when I have to do it. But I love that I can.)

Those little things were incredibly important to me. Things I had taken for granted my whole life: the ability to shop, make a meal, wash dishes, vacuum, play with my kids, read a book, walk up the stairs, go an entire day without a headache, smile and mean it, take a walk and marvel at the sunset.

Little things I hope I never take for granted again.

And then there were the big things.

5

In Case You Didn't Know, Healing is a Nonlinear Process

What Progress Sometimes Looked Like

Progress finally started to feel real a year after my first myofascial release session. For one thing, in January, I was able to get a part-time job. That was good for me in many ways: it got me out of the house during the day, and going back to work gave me a sense of capability and function. I was teaching music in two elementary schools, working about 14 hours a week. It was just enough to not be completely exhausted. I would take a short nap during any breaks I got, and when I got off work at noon on Friday, I would drive to Utah for my weekly appointment. I was spending much of my paycheck on weekly travel and therapy sessions, but the progress was visible. I was working again!

Then in February of that year, I attended the John Barnes Myofascial Release Healing Seminar in Sedona, Arizona as both a client and patient. I went hoping to find things that might help me progress further in my journey, perhaps even a kind of healing that would allow me to eventually stop driving to Utah each week for help. The brochure spoke about enhancing my healing path and helping my treatment sessions be more effective, of developing the ability to better tune into my body and self-treat. It spoke of learning how to eliminate my pain.

Much like the internal something that kept me going back to treatment each week, there was an internal something pushing me toward attending that healing seminar.

> *February 14, 2015*
>
> *"I thought a lot about it for a long time and did a lot of research on how to get there and where to stay. Did a lot of asking myself what I wanted most and what would be best for me on this trip. Did a lot of letting things just...sit. And then I made my plans. It took a lot of work and a lot of courage for me to make some of those phone calls to put everything in place. But ever since I did that part, I have really been looking forward to this, because I know it is something I need. Things have fallen into place in the kind of way that lets me know that yes, this is what I need to do.*
>
> *Things were good until yesterday when I picked up the rental car. Now I have this fairly constant and very critical dialogue running in my head: 'This is too expensive... I don't really need to go... I didn't plan well... It won't be worth it... I am not worth it...' The dialogue goes on and on, but that's the general idea. And I know it isn't true. Want so very much to believe it isn't true. Am trying to hold on to how I felt when I was making my plans. But this dialogue is loud..."*

I had just started my part-time job, and my husband had not yet moved from Mississippi to join us in Idaho. Going to the seminar was not at all convenient or easy. I didn't have any paid time off, plus it took a lot of arranging to provide care for my children during that time. I had never driven to Arizona before and felt like I was making this journey all alone. Which just made it that much harder.

But I went.

And am so glad I did.

It was another pivot point for me.

I would love to be able to say I was healed at that seminar, but I wasn't. Not even close. Not much of what was taught sank in very deeply, either. I was in a lot of physical pain by the time I arrived at the seminar, and it was difficult for me to sit in the chairs. My 14-hour drive (Mapquest had told me to expect 10 to 11 hours) had prompted the sensation of a piece of rebar being shoved into my brain to return, and my back was aching and my body was tightening up. I ended up sitting on the floor against the wall at the edge of the group because that was the least uncomfortable place for me to sit.

I sat there and cried during most of the seminar. I hurt. I was tired. It was difficult to pay attention. Practicing the techniques we were being taught made me hurt more. By the end of the second day, I had to sit out the activities because I had just too pain in my neck and back and shoulders to hold someone's legs. I was hurting and frustrated and alone and wondering why I was there.

While I was at the seminar, I also had two therapy sessions at the John Barnes treatment center in Sedona, called Therapy on the Rocks. That just made me feel worse. Much like Michael and John had done, my therapist asked questions I couldn't answer in ways that caused me to shut down inside. Again, I was angry, defensive, scared, braced.

It was not the help I had been hoping for when I planned that trip. But it was the help I needed.

I knew by the time the seminar was over that I wanted to be a therapist. I knew even *before* the seminar was over that I wanted to be a therapist.

The questions that made me so angry and frustrated during my time at Therapy on the Rocks are ones that have stuck with me. And not because I stayed angry about them—they stayed with me because I gradually realized that the answers were stepping-stones in my understanding of myself.

Five months after I returned from that first seminar, I enrolled in massage school. A year later, I was back in Sedona to begin training as a myofascial release therapist.

Those were some of the high points.

What Progress Other Times Looked Like...Or Put Another Way, Setbacks

There were also plenty of low points during that second year. Most of them seemed to revolve around continuing my therapy. Instead of my therapy visits becoming less frequent, I discovered that I actually needed treatment more often, so I started scheduling two-hour sessions to make the most of my travel time. Sometimes it seemed like the first hour was spent undoing the stress and tensions of the week and the time I had just spent traveling, and the second hour was spent trying to make some progress. Or sometimes the first hour was spent waiting for me to unbrace and be willing to be there, and the second was spent trying to undo the week's stresses. Sometimes the entire two hours were spent with me braced and having a conversation in my head about what I was feeling but wasn't going to say. Either way, most of the time it seemed like we were just putting out the same fire every week with maybe a half-step forward tossed into the mix. Sometimes not even that.

So I started scheduling two or three appointments per trip to Utah, sometimes staying overnight to get additional treatment before returning home. Eventually, I stayed for an entire week to do some intensive treatments of multiple sessions per day for several days. That's when I really started to learn about embracing the healing response that often comes with myofascial release.

A word of warning: if you are going to wind up feeling discouraged, it is most likely to happen during a healing crisis. It is called healing "crisis" for a reason, because it can feel like the lowest point of your existence sometimes.

You see, something marvelous and awful (and sometimes incredibly hard to wrap the brain around) happens when your body shifts into healing: you start to feel all of the things you haven't been feeling. And that might make things seem like you have suddenly taken a huge step backwards, because things seem suddenly worse.

I frequently felt that way. And it took time to really sink in that those moments actually *weren't* bad—they weren't undoing progress or taking me backwards or making things worse. My body was simply going through the chaos of reorganization. Things were changing on a deeper level.

But it sure felt like I was doing something wrong! I've had more sessions than I can count where I was left feeling like I'd been walloped and run over by a truck. And that's saying it nicely. I've gone home and slept for hours, taken a few days to slowly move through feeling exhausted and sore and achy all over, and then gone back for another session. And then come home and slept for hours.

I've barely been able to drive to some sessions and completely unable to drive home afterward. I've sat in the parking lot for a long time, sometimes sleeping, sometimes crying and feeling sorry for myself, sometimes simply doing my best to stay present and keep breathing, to allow my body to feel through what is changing. Sometimes I've needed a ride from a friend because it became apparent that I would not be driving anywhere for a bit because movement kept bringing waves of pain that were so intense I felt nauseous. Sometimes my brain doesn't work too well after a session, and I feel like I shouldn't even be trying to walk, much less drive. Moving with about as much speed and grace as a drunken turtle moving through that peanut butter.

At times, I've been unable to sleep following some intense changes. I've been awake all night, experiencing shifting and changes that brought up old and familiar pain. Cycling through shivering, chills, fever, and flu-like symptoms until dawn, when I could finally fall into an exhausted sleep. Times when I have felt my way through the tissue memory and sensations of past illnesses and surgeries, childbirth, and a miscarriage. Times I have spent curled up in a corner with a blanket as waves of emotion and pain washed through me. Sessions that were followed by intense feelings of depression and despair when I wondered if I would ever feel good again. Or stop crying.

Once, I was at a seminar in Delaware with friends. Much of the treatment one particular day focused on the pelvis and sacrum. All good, I thought...until I was having a great deal of pain and trouble sitting by the end of the day, and I could barely stand. Walking had become a hesitant and painful shuffle. I hadn't felt that way in years! Going down the stairs to the car was really, really slow, and going up the stairs to my room on the third floor of the house where we were staying was an impossibility. I laid on the floor in the sitting room of the first floor for several hours, letting my pelvis soften and continue to shift while my friends went out to dinner.

It is never (then or now) pleasant.

It is definitely not easy.

It is rarely convenient.

And it didn't always make a lot of sense to the logical, rational part of my brain that was screaming at me, "Something must be wrong! Things are worse now! Stop!!"

It wasn't. They weren't. I didn't.

It. Was. ALL. Good.

Every bit of it, even when it felt awful.

Sometimes things felt so ridiculously bad that it was almost humorous. I can now look back on those things and remember how ridiculously bad they were at the time and laugh about them. I learned that those things would pass. And that what I resisted feeling would only persist. That those things were all already there inside of me, deep in my tissues. And that the healing would come as I allowed myself to feel.

The process took trust. And gentleness with myself. It took learning to trust the intuitive part of me that whispers quietly inside that everything is okay. That this is an important and necessary part of the process. That the only way out is through. That I could and still can do this. It took gentleness when I would start to berate and judge myself for feeling how I was feeling and wishing it would all just go away. Gentleness when I started to beat myself up for starting down this path in the first place. For opening the can of worms, the Pandora's box of problems and issues. Gentleness every time I have been in that place of feeling so much worse, when the doubt starts to creep in, insisting that things will not only never change but that now I have made them worse...

I did not learn any of that quickly, but it did really start to sink in during that second year. And I found myself in a sort of love/hate relationship as I learned to embrace it rather than fight it.

There have been a lot of setbacks as I learned (and am often still reminded of) that particular lesson.

The setback I was most unprepared for came later that fall. Massage school was difficult on me, both physically and mentally. Although school had always been easy for me in the past, now I found myself struggling to concentrate and remember things. It was as if my body and brain didn't really start to wake up and engage until close to lunchtime, and even then, I felt sluggish mentally and physically. I was having to focus and learn in a much different way than what I was used to. It was definitely not the easy learning I had always experienced in school; now it required great mental effort to comprehend and digest the material.

Sitting for four hours of class in the morning was an issue; I was always stretching and moving, rarely holding still. When my head or body was really aching, I would sometimes stand at the back of the classroom.

But I could deal with those things. The bigger problem was that the bodywork practice in class was causing my body to tense and brace again. Touch was already painful to me, and after only about a month or so in school, it was becoming even more painful, to the point that there was some concern about my ability to complete the program.

Eventually, I was diagnosed with fibromyalgia.

After all of the work and time and effort and tears and money, I was diagnosed with something that seemed insurmountable. The school recommended that I take a year off. "Come back when you feel better," they told me. But I couldn't. That deep knowing inside knew that if I quit, I would never come back. I also knew what I wanted to do with my life and career and that I needed that license.

Bless the administrative staff of the school who listened and believed me when I said I could finish! I stayed in school with some modifications to bodywork practice in class, and I continued driving to Utah once a week to undo the tension that would build up in between visits. It felt like I was right back to putting out the same fires over and over again with maybe a bit of progress in between.

With this new label of fibromyalgia stuck to me, I didn't know how I would ever be able to practice as a therapist...but I still kept showing up.

Part 3: Healing. . . Healing. . . Healed!

6

What Does That Really Mean? And Now What?!

Perhaps it is a huge leap to go from a diagnosis of fibromyalgia to "healed and recovered." It definitely was *not* the short jump represented here from one section of a book to the next. (Don't even begin to think healing was easy or quick!)

By the time I was diagnosed, though, I had had enough experience with myofascial release to know that I would be okay. And I was, even in those times when things still got really bad. Because more than anything, I had learned that healing is a process, not an event.

Healing didn't occur in some magical therapy session where something was finally touched on and released in a way it never had been before, making me suddenly better. (Although I did occasionally hope healing could be that simple.)

Healing didn't happen as my body started to adjust and things began to pop back into place for the first time: sacrum, vertebrae, the bones in my feet... They often popped right back out because I needed the repetition of going back and forth between feeling lousy and feeling great as my body more fully integrated change.

Healing didn't happen overnight; I didn't wake up one morning just fine, like a child with appendicitis who wakes up all better after the appendectomy.

Healing happened in the in-between.

I don't even know exactly when or how everything changed, because it has been the accumulation of a million different things. Often seemingly small and insignificant things. Treatment sessions, questions asked, things held on to and over time explored, painful tissue memories felt through, old beliefs and stories examined, new beliefs and behaviors put in their place. Hundreds of hours of myofascial release therapy. Thousands of dollars spent. Tens of thousands of road miles on my car. Hours and hours of sleepless nights. Binders full of journal entries. Too many emails to my therapist to count.

In a slow way—so slow I didn't even notice sometimes—all of those things started to accumulate, and I began to feel much better.

As an emerging myofascial release therapist, I started my formal training with John Barnes and his staff. That first year of seminars was tough; during those trainings, it often felt like every issue I had ever had mentally, emotionally, or physically would be exposed, seen, shaken up, and stirred around. Eleven days at a time of that, and I would frequently feel like a hot mess! I kept wondering how I was ever going to be a therapist when I was in so much need of help myself.

Eventually, though, I did graduate from massage school and open my own practice as a myofascial release therapist. It was slow going at first. Not because I didn't have clients, but because I did not have the strength and energy to see too many.

I started off seeing one or two clients a week, then gradually built up to one or two clients a day: see one in the morning, take a nap, and then see another in the afternoon. Eventually, I got to where I could work two or three days a week while reserving my Fridays (and sometimes Thursdays) to go to Utah for my own continued treatment.

And I continued to make progress, sometimes even in leaps and bounds. And eventually, I found that life is what is lived during and after and in between all of the ups and downs. I thought that to be "healed" would mean I would not hurt again, that the aches and pains and sleepless nights and internal chatter and worry would be gone. It doesn't.

The ups and downs are the process of life. They are life. And trying to hold out for and create a life without those ups and downs would give me a life I would not actually enjoy.

Somewhere along the way, I forgot that chronic pain was once a thing. I was seeing as many clients as I cared to in my own clinic, and rather than putting out fires in my own treatment sessions, I was making progress. My pelvis had gradually become more aligned and mobile. My headaches ceased long ago. And I was (and still am) rebuilding strength and confidence in my entire body.

Healing truly is a process, not an event.

Five years into the process, I know I am healed. And "healed" does not mean that I do not sometimes have aches and pains. It does not mean that I do not experience healing responses or that I have stopped receiving myofascial release treatment regularly.

Healing does mean that I am more at peace with myself and no longer feel small and threatened inside. I'm no longer hiding from myself or others. I feel more at ease in my life.

Healing means that I have learned (or am comfortable continuing to learn) how to negotiate and respond to all that life brings without the clenching and bracing that got me into trouble in the first place.

I am creating a life I no longer want to run away from.

Renegotiation

We all assume (or maybe just *I* have assumed) that the body knows how to work correctly. The heart knows how to pump blood. The lungs know how to expand and fill with oxygen. The body knows what to do with the oxygen it receives and knows where it needs to go. The stomach knows how to digest food, the cells know how to distribute nutrients, etc.

Only what I have found is that—if it gets stuck for long enough—eventually, the body can forget how to do what should come naturally.

Mine forgot that movement was safe. Forgot that connection and curiosity and exploration were safe. Forgot what balanced and open and unrestricted felt like.

By the time I found the right help, to my body, being "normal" meant being tight, pulled in, clenched, braced.

By the time I found the right help, I had a pelvis that was rotated and tilted forward, a spine that was sitting on an unstable base and holding on as tightly as possible to stabilize the rest of me, a torso and shoulders that had shifted askew on top of my spine, and my head trying to balance atop all of that.

All my body knew to do was tighten and brace wherever and whenever possible in an effort to hold me all together. No wonder movement became unsafe and dizziness was my norm! No wonder I was in so much pain and was so exhausted—all of that clenching and bracing internally required so much energy! Energy I wasn't consciously aware of expending but that was very much being expended.

I had what I considered to be an "energy budget" for the day, and I was constantly monitoring it and checking the balance against the cost of what I wanted to do. I called that negotiating with myself.

Want to go to a movie later with my husband? That's going to require the ability to sit for a few hours. A quick check-in with myself... Nope, can't do that tonight—I've already used up my energy for the day by going for a walk in the morning and putting something in the crockpot for dinner. My body is aching too much from those activities to go to the movies and sit for that long.

My daughter would really like me to come watch her volleyball game? It's at 11:00 a.m. Oh, good! That's not terribly early—it gives me time to wake up slowly or sleep in a bit if it has been a particularly restless night. The trade-off might be that I need a nap afterward. Or I might need to lie on the bleachers for a while to ease my back.

This type of negotiating went on for a long time. What I gradually started to realize, though, was that somehow, my energy budget was increasing. Activities were often still exhausting and painful....but I was gaining the ability to do more of them within the same energy cycle.

As the tissues in my body continued to unstick and unglue themselves, the alignment of my joints and bones improved, and the energy I had unknowingly been using to hold myself so tightly together could be used for other things, including curiosity and exploration.

As that happened, I began renegotiating with my body about all the things I had wondered if I would ever be able to do again.

Redefining and Losing Labels

In those early months and years of myofascial release treatment, the thing I was most concerned about was pain relief. And also regaining a sense of capability in my life. Being able to walk normally again.

And gradually, I did start to regain those things. But obviously, the process was not as simple as I had thought or hoped it would be. Somewhere in my mind, I had the idea that when I was "better," I would have my life back: I would be able to do the things I used to do in the way I used to do them. I would be recovered. I talked in terms of The Things I Had Lost. I wanted those things back.

But that meant learning to negotiate with my body as I regained my activities. I had frequent conversations with myself about the stress levels, frequency, and duration of any activity, from going for a short walk or going grocery shopping to going out on a date with my husband. I had to learn to really listen to the signals my body was sending and begin to interpret what they meant (and often differently than I had in the past).

I learned that "experiencing pain" doesn't always mean "stop doing the activity." Any more than "recovery" means "never hurting again."

Discovering that there were a couple of problems with my initial hopes and beliefs about recovery was a tough pill to swallow.

One of them was that the very life I claimed to want back so badly—or, more accurately, the life*style* I wanted back—was the very lifestyle and mentality that had landed me where I was. I couldn't go back to doing the things the way I had been doing them without ending up, eventually, right back in chronic pain.

That was an incredibly difficult concept for me to comprehend. If recovery wasn't getting my life back, then what was it? If I wasn't going to go back to doing the things I had been doing, then what was I going to do??

Then I realized it wasn't so much about the things I was doing in that former life as it was about *how* I was doing them.

Again, another difficult concept for me to comprehend.

The other problem with my view of recovery was that every setback became a mental and emotional challenge. If I was recovering, why was I hurting again? If I was recovering, why did things often seem worse? If I was recovering, why did life still seem so hard?

I've been through many layers. And I've found I still don't always have answers to those questions, especially when asked by someone who views recovery differently than I now do.

Was recovery when the headache stopped? When the pounding, throbbing pain in the base of my skull was no longer my constant companion? When I eventually realized that the headache had gradually disappeared without my even being aware of its disappearance, I felt like I had made a huge step in my progress. But I still felt far from recovered, because I still couldn't easily do the things I used to do.

Was recovery when my husband could lightly hold my hand in his and I didn't feel like I was being squeezed in a fiery, painful vice?

Was recovery when I went back to work? Did part-time work count? Or was I not recovered until I went back to work full-time? Did it count if working exhausted me? Or did I have to be able to work a full-time job with ease before I could consider myself recovered?

Was I recovered when I started sleeping again? Or felt awareness return to my legs? Or felt like I was walking normally again? These things were nice, and again, they were huge milestones in my journey. But I was still monitoring how life was affecting my body. Struggling with flare-ups, struggling on the days I felt sluggish and foggy-brained and drained of energy, struggling when small tasks seemed insurmountable because of the fatigue. It wasn't all the time anymore, no, but I didn't consider myself to be "better," either.

Every time I *have* felt better, I have started to reach for more. It's not enough to not hurt all the time or to be able to work. I want to live! I want to move. Be active. Run. Jump. Play. Laugh. Stay up late at night and watch silly movies with my kids. Hike in the snow. Travel. Love. Chronic pain robbed me of many of those things—the ability to do them, the ability to enjoy them.

So I kept reaching (and still do). I kept improving and maintaining and then moving forward and improving some more. And every time I did take a step forward, it seemed like more issues would show up...and I would be back to monitoring myself and worrying about my activity levels and wondering if I was regressing.

No matter how good things get, constantly monitoring how activities affect me is *not* recovery.

Eventually, I found it was actually my definition of recovery that was getting in my way. My belief about what "recovery" meant was causing me problems. I thought recovery and being healed meant I would never hurt again, that I could use and enjoy my body without pain.

It sounds silly now, but that's what I thought I was able to do before that Saturday morning when my life took a drastic detour from what I had planned. I didn't realize that what I had lost most was my ability to respond appropriately to how my body was feeling. Didn't realize that I had lost the ability to trust my own instincts with regards to what my body could and couldn't do. Didn't realize that I didn't really feel pain because I was numbing out. Didn't realize I had come to identify myself by the labels of "chronic pain" and "fibromyalgia."

And that there was a part of me—no matter how good I felt—that was always worried about regressing, always keeping tabs on activities and protecting me from things my subconscious believed would put me right back where I had been.

But recovery isn't never hurting, never feeling pain in the body.

First, recovery was losing my identification of myself as someone with fibromyalgia. That was absolutely essential to do. Until then, most of my world sounded like "I can't run anymore because I have fibromyalgia" or "My body hurts when I hike because I have fibromyalgia" or "I'm not sleeping well because I have fibromyalgia" or "Don't ask me to try and remember anything, because I have fibromyalgia and I can't."

I structured my life, limited my activities, explained my behavior, and defined myself in terms of a diagnostic label.

Only, I am not that label.

Losing my identification with it was one of the first recoveries I experienced. It happened without my even noticing it—I wasn't actively denying it or using positive affirmations to avoid what I was feeling. One day, I simply realized that I no longer considered myself to have fibromyalgia. Did I still hurt? Yep. Have flare-ups? Yep. Bad days? Still yep. But did I identify myself as "someone who has fibromyalgia"?

No.

I had recovered my sense of self.

I am not my symptoms.

I am not a diagnosis.

I am simply me.

It was a subtle shift, one I didn't even recognize until the week I started to do research on fibromyalgia for a project at work.

I started reading the available literature to see what people struggling with chronic pain are currently being told. I joined a few fibromyalgia support groups on Facebook and followed them for a week or so. I read some blogs written by people sharing stories of their journey.

And I quickly fell into a hole of depression.

I started identifying with the symptoms: I started remembering the brain fog and the joint pain and the fatigue, started identifying with the mindset, started feeling sorry for myself, moving more slowly, gradually pulling inward in order to protect myself from hurting when I moved. Remembered what it felt like to be told there was no cure; remembered how it hit me like a ton of bricks to be told fibromyalgia was something I would have for the rest of my life, that people don't get better from it but that the symptoms can be managed. Remembered the discussions about my limitations and how medications might help.

I watched the participants in the Facebook group identify with their diagnostic labels. Watched their discussions of how difficult life was, how painful, how hopeless...and momentarily got dragged back in. It was painful, and it was a scary slide. For a moment, I once again believed I could not, was not actually healing from fibromyalgia.

What I read over those few weeks was convincing enough to drop me into a deep hole of self-pity for a few days. To make me question what I had experienced.

Until I looked around at where I was and where I had been. And remembered: yes, I had recovered.

I finished my research and got out of those support groups as fast as I could.

It surprised me to feel how quickly I started to believe what I was reading in spite of all my experiences. It saddened me to see how many people truly feel there is no hope for recovery. I wonder how that might change if the dialogue about what it takes to heal changed. I wonder how things might be different for people if we stopped identifying each other by diagnostic labels. A set of symptoms is not who we are.

I remember the day I was with a client and we were discussing her struggles with chronic pain. She asked me a question about my own journey and how I was dealing with fibromyalgia. I had a moment of complete confusion...what she was referring to? Had a blank look on my face for just a moment.

And then I remembered: oh, yeah! I did have that. I had forgotten it was once a thing. You know you have recovered from something when you forget it was actually once a thing. Life had gotten that good.

Recovering Trust in Myself

The other element crucial to my recovery was regaining my sense of trust in myself. For a little while, letting go of the labels of chronic pain and fibromyalgia was actually kind of a scary thing to do, because I could no longer use them as a reason or an excuse as to why I couldn't do things. I didn't realize how much of a safety blanket those labels had become. They were something to hide behind, something to define me. If *they* no longer defined me, that meant that *I* had to start to define myself.

Which meant learning to trust myself again.

Initially, that meant learning to trust my physical senses and trust that I could respond appropriately to what I was feeling.

There is a lot of contradictory information out there about movement and activity: how to train, how to build up strength, what the best method is for relaxation, why and when to push through things, why and when *not* to push through things.

Of all the things I needed most to recover, trusting what I feel and sense was possibly the most important—without it, every setback would send me into a temporary spiral, would make me wonder if I was reaching for too much.

Aches and pains associated with activities that others might consider to be normal are huge danger signs to my brain. Movement that requires muscle tension to initiate and carry out often also causes pain. When someone says to "not push past pain" with a movement, my brain doesn't know how to translate that since I hurt to begin with.

There hasn't been a lot of help available in navigating these particular waters. I've had to learn to trust my own internal sense.

Aches and pains after activities that many people might consider to be normal were also huge danger signs to my brain. Learning to process them has been a journey of its own sort. As I have started to move more, I have become very aware of the hold my subconscious has on my movement, and I have had to do a lot of neuro-muscular re-education. Essentially, I've had to retrain my brain to recognize activity as safe, retrain my brain to not tell my body to clench and brace, that there is no need to protect.

I get a lot of internal chatter about that sometimes, chatter that can be very loud and very convincing. Entire conversations go on inside about how something will affect my body and why I can't do something. If I listen to those conversations, my muscles tighten and tense in response to my brain signaling that something needs protection. This usually happens long before I even ever attempt the activity.

I readily acknowledge that sometimes my brain should not be in charge—it can be neurotic in its need to keep me safe. I have learned to recognize the deeper, internal wisdom I have in me that knows better.

Our bodies are capable of far more than we have ever been allowed to believe.

Our bodies are capable of far more than *we* allow ourselves to believe.

It has been essential for me to reclaim my trust in my own internal sense of what my body can and cannot do. That seems to be a constant learning process and something I am continually refining. I frequently know by the tension in my body that I am listening to the wrong voices and that I need to take a minute to quiet myself mentally and tune into the intuitive, instinctive part of my nature.

It takes trust in oneself to do that.

And like everything else in this journey of recovery, gaining that trust has been a process. It doesn't just happen. I didn't wake up one day and decide I wasn't going to argue with myself about things or tie myself into knots inside trying to figure things out. I didn't suddenly stop running through all of the ways things might go wrong and sifting through numerous scenarios in my head in an effort to avoid all of the potential dangers before attempting to make a decision. My brain didn't stop its constant chatter.

What did happen is that I gained an understanding of what was going on inside and the tools and experiences I needed to navigate through and negotiate with myself. Like everything else, it has taken a lot of repetition for this truth to sink in: I can trust what I feel. Not what I think. What I *feel.*

Recovery absolutely required learning to trust what I feel.

Part 4: Lessons Learned

7

Examining What I Think I Know About Myself

As my physical issues gradually changed and improved, I would often run into stuck places, things that just didn't seem to change no matter how much treatment I received. Throughout my slow and thorough process, I gradually learned that often there is a mentality holding a physicality in place. The physical issues cannot and will not change until the mentality holding them in place does.

For me, that's where self-examination really started to come into play.

One of the questions I have been asked—and one that I return to frequently myself—is "What if who you think you are is not who you are meant to be?"

I mean, really, if you're honest, how *do* you think of yourself? On your good days? On your bad days? What words do you use to describe yourself when talking to others? To your friends? To those you want to impress? To yourself when you look in the mirror? What do you wish you were but think you are not? What or who do you think you are but may not actually be? Or maybe are not *meant* to be?

And how is your body physically responding to what you are saying?

Perhaps I am the only one who has had issues with this. If I am being honest, I have spent great portions of my life wanting to be something other than what I was: smarter or faster or lighter or braver, taller and thinner, a better mom, a better student, a better wife. I wanted to be less angry, more calm, more gentle. I wanted to be not always viewing myself in a negative light.

In general, when I took the time to pause and assess what I saw and felt, I did not like myself much of the time.

I didn't know that was affecting my physically.

My therapist, Michael, would frequently comment on how down I was on myself. How hard I was on myself. How heavy the expectations were for myself that I always carried around with me, expectations that I always had to figure things out, that I *needed* to figure things out. He would ask, "What if you could drop just that one thing?" What if it was okay to act on what I was feeling? What if it's okay to feel jealousy or anger? Or to feel small and stepped on? What if I could just *not* know? What if I don't have to figure anything out?

And the biggest question of them all: what if all of those things I thought I was supposed to do or be were not at all what I was meant to do or be?

That question has gradually been answered over time as I have realized that I am not who I thought I was. And just like all the other things, it has been a nuanced question that could only be answered by gaining many layers of understanding, understanding I have been gaining as I've learned the lessons I needed to learn in order for true healing to occur.

I found that much of the pain I was experiencing was caused by clenching and bracing, and much of *that* was caused by the things I was thinking and believing. About myself. About others. About how the world operates.

When I say "what I believed," I'm not talking about religion. I am talking about the underlying stories each of us has playing out in the background of our lives, constantly explaining what things mean.

For example, if someone yells at me, my brain has an explanation about what that means. My body then responds to this belief, this story. When someone yells at me, I immediately feel like I have done something wrong, and my body clenches and pulls inward just a bit to protect myself. That's what I mean by beliefs. In this instance, at some point in my life, I developed the belief that being yelled at means I am in trouble and have done something wrong that I need to be ashamed of. Because of that belief, every time I hear yelling, I clench. Eventually, all of that clenching leads to distorting and tugging and pulling in the fascial tissue of the body, and that leads to pain.

While that belief may have served me at some point, it no longer does. Yelling may not at all mean what I made it out to be—it could be a warning of danger, for example, or it could be someone trying to get my attention from across the room. Yelling could be an indication of surprise or excitement. It doesn't necessarily mean that I've done something wrong.

In order to truly and completely heal, I have had to unearth every one of the beliefs that was limiting how I interacted with myself and others, beliefs that were affecting my physical, emotional, and mental reactions to life. I've had to dig them out. Examine them. Change the story where needed. And then toss out the rest.

As difficult as the physical aspects of myofascial release have been, digging out the beliefs has almost been harder.

But examining my beliefs has also been the most necessary part of the process.

I've learned that when things seem stuck, it is often the beliefs that need to be examined, because the physicality cannot change until the mentality holding it in place also changes.

This is where some of the most important and memorable lessons lie.

8

If I Treated My Car the Way I Treated Myself. . .

I talked earlier about the things I had ignored. Some were emotional, but most were physical things I am aware of that had affected my body. There have been deeper forces at work, though, tying me into knots, beating me up inside. On some level, all of that was my own doing.

If I treated my car the way I treated myself, it would have stopped running long ago. All of the trying to change and wishing things were different were the equivalent of trying to replace and exchange engine parts with no comprehension whatsoever of how the engine works to begin with.

Yep, that's what I was trying to do.

Early on, I found out that myofascial release treatment sessions were often the place where a pebble would be kicked, a pebble that at some later time would become an avalanche. Sometimes, the pebble was a physical change, but more often, it was a mental change. A change and shift in understanding. I've needed to repeat and repeat and repeat seeing just how poorly I was treating myself and how that needed to change. That pebble got kicked around a *lot* before the avalanche of understanding occurred.

April 12, 2015

"Sometimes, the very things that we think are useless and broken are actually making life run well. Sometimes, the very things we think we don't need are what we discard and throw away, things that are essential for proper functioning.

My van key broke last week—the plastic casing that the metal key part attaches to completely fell apart. But I had another broken key that was no longer attached to a key ring, and thought that I might be able to combine the two broken keys to make one whole key. I unscrewed both cases and swapped what needed to be swapped. While I was doing that, the circuit board that has never functioned fell out of each key. The plastic casing on my key has buttons to unlock and lock the van and even an automatic ignition button that we were told had been disabled years ago. These buttons have never worked in the 10 years we have owned the van.

The circuit board had gunk on it, and the battery was corroded. I thought it was useless. Since it was difficult to fit back into the key, I threw it away.

We do that sometimes with things we think are useless or that don't function as we think they should. We do that with relationships, with our jobs, with our hopes and dreams and goals. With ourselves. We figuratively clean house and throw out the things that no longer work...only sometimes maybe we discard things that are actually essential. We just can't see how something has been functioning all along. That's what happened with my van key.

A few hours later, I went outside, got in the van to go pick a child up from school, put the key in the ignition, and turned it. The engine wouldn't turn over. It tried to, but it just couldn't, because—unknown to me—that circuit board has something in it that allows the engine to start. Without it, my van will not run. I didn't know this for several hours, not until after my husband had called somebody to see if they could come help. Not until after those two men had tried their best and left feeling badly about the unfortunate fact was that the best they could do for me was tow the van somewhere if we decided to take it to a mechanic. Not until I remembered that earlier that day, I had thrown away something I thought was useless because I hadn't realized it was essential.

Much later that evening, I dug the gunky circuit board and its corroded battery out of the bottom of the trash. Unscrewed the key case again. Worked a bit at getting the circuit board into its proper place. Reassembled the key. When I went out to try it in the van, it started just fine.

I needed this lesson. It wasn't about the van—it was about learning to not be too quick to discard things. And I am not talking about the clutter and junk in the house, although that could also apply. I am talking about not being too quick to judge and label people and things as useless in our lives. About learning to listen carefully to all that is said when help is offered. One particular phrase during my conversation with the men who were trying to start my van sparked the memory of what I had thrown away that afternoon: "I don't know who works on newer vehicles! They are all so computerized." These kind men were saying that as they were leaving and feeling like they hadn't helped. But that was what I needed to hear to fix what I had done.

This lesson was about recognizing that sometimes we are actually the cause of many of the problems we encounter. This lesson was about fixing things quickly when we become aware of our mistakes and being grateful that the message was heard on Tuesday night instead of after the garbage had been picked up on Thursday morning. Who am I to judge something or someone as being useless and unnecessary? That supposedly 'useless' thing or person may be the very thing or person that's helping something else function really well, and I might just not be aware of it.

I call this lesson 'the parable of the van key,' and I remember it every time I start my vehicle."

At the time, this lesson applied to the people and things in my life that I was dealing with. The realization that I was causing problems for myself took time to sink in, that I was discounting and trying to discard parts of myself that didn't seem to be working, parts that seemed to be covered with gunk and corroded and useless. Some of the following chapters give more descriptions of just how hard I tried to change things that turned out to not need changing at all.

There is no part of me that does not have a place and a purpose. I am still learning that. Still finding parts that I don't quite know what to do with. But at least I'm no longer trying to rip them out or replace them—instead, I'm doing my best to allow them to be and waiting to see what they do, how they best function, and what they need in order to best function.

That was the first lesson: stop throwing away bits and pieces of myself without any understanding of what they are and what they can do.

The other lesson has been about reframing what I have considered to be limitations. In June of 2015, I left on a trip and didn't return for 19 days. I was wandering. Eventually, my wanderings took me through 13 states and more than 4,000 miles. It was a great trip for many reasons, one of them being that it was the first long trip I had taken alone since my world fell apart. In a way, it was a test of what I could do, wanted to be able to do, and thought I should be able to do without difficulty.

June 15, 2015

"We all have limitations. I know this. At least, my head says it knows this. So why am I still struggling with the frustration that I cannot do everything I think I am supposed to do or think I want to do? Why do I keep thinking that I need to be everything to everyone, even when sometimes I don't really want to be? And when I am not, why do I keep beating myself up and telling myself I am a failure? Or feeling disappointed and telling myself I need to try harder, to do better?

I say I understand and accept that we all have limitations, including a limited amount of time and energy and resources each day. I say I accept this, but I think I must accept this only if my limits are well beyond all that I want to accomplish. I am struggling to feel like I have done my best if I hit my limit before everything is done even as a part of me points out the obvious fact that everything will never be done.

I got a highly personalized learning experience this weekend to help me understand a little bit more about what the concept of limitations might really mean to me.

I drove a little silver Honda Civic across the country last week. Spent some time in the south with my daughter and then put her on a plane before heading home myself. Went from Mississippi up into Wyoming in two days. What a great trip! Got awesome gas mileage, too, along with a very memorable lesson.

York, Nebraska was about 720 miles into my trip along I-80 west, and that's where I stopped the first night. Slept fairly well. Filled up the car with gas the next morning and headed out toward Cheyenne, Wyoming. If you have ever driven along I-80 across Nebraska, you know there's a lot of beautiful wide-open space where the green of the fields meets the clouds and the sky. But there are few towns, which means few places to get fuel. I have driven this route many times. I know this. But I hadn't driven this route in this particular vehicle.

On the first day, I stopped every 200 miles or so for gas and a quick break. It felt like I was stopping a lot even though really I only stopped four times that day. On the second day, I wanted to go a little farther before stopping. Based on the gas mileage I had been getting and the amount of fuel I put in each time I stopped, I figured I safely could go at least 350 miles before needing to refuel. So off I went. Had a goal. Had a plan.

At about 200 miles, I passed a travel stop. I like those—they generally have lots of fuel pumps and clean bathrooms. But I wasn't ready to stop yet. When I travel alone, I check in with my inner self frequently, and I did this as I approached the travel stop. Did I need to refuel? I didn't think I did and I didn't really want to stop yet, but checked in with myself to see if this was okay. The thought came back that I might want to stop and get it out of the way, but I assured myself it would be okay if I went a little farther, so I kept going.

Another 50 miles, another travel stop. I thought about getting off there for gas, but I had just entered a construction zone and didn't want the hassle of getting back onto the interstate if I got off of it. It wasn't really a big deal—just my excuse to keep going. When I checked in with my inner self, this time, I heard, 'You might want to get gas here even though it is a bit inconvenient. But if you don't, you will still be okay. You will just need to stop soon.'

I had a goal and I wasn't quite ready to stop. Thought it would be nice to go a little farther. I was making good time! As I passed the exit, I was reasoning and rationalizing and remembering from a previous trip that another nice rest stop should be 'not too far ahead.' Plus, I still had 100 miles' worth of road in the tank.

At 280 miles, I started paying attention to signs signaling upcoming cities. I would be passing Sidney, Nebraska when I had gone 300 miles. The only reason I had ever stopped in Sidney was because it has a Walmart that's highly visible and easily accessible from the interstate. Sidney has lousy gas stations, though—more than once during the many trips my family and I made across the country, my husband and children heard me say I will never stop in Sidney for gas again.

And I sure wasn't going to this time, either. I didn't need Walmart, and I had told myself I didn't like getting gas there. Besides, it was always more expensive. I checked in with my inner self as Sidney came closer, and this time I heard, 'How stubborn are you going to be?'

That made me start to chuckle to myself, because I can be pretty stubborn. So I answered myself, saying, 'I am not stopping here. I still have 50 miles to find a gas station.' This time, my inner self let me know that I would be okay...but I that might wish I had stopped there. I heard the 'You will be okay part' and passed the exit to Sidney...and thought little about the 'You might wish you had' part as I kept going.

And kept going. And going. No visible gas station at the next exit. Nothing at the next one, either, or the next. The next town was at least a mile off the interstate. I was starting to get a little tense; I could feel it in my solar plexus, in my jaw. Had to remind myself to relax and tell myself, 'It will be okay.' Still, I started reviewing where I could have stopped, started to second-guess my choices. But hadn't my inner self said I would be okay? Yes, she had. . .but what did that really mean?

The gas gauge started to drop below empty as I went up some of the hills. I started to wonder if 'being okay' meant I was going to learn an awesome lesson as I ran out of gas on the interstate because I hadn't thought I needed to stop, hadn't wanted to stop, and had just been plain too stubborn to stop. But all I could do at that point was keep driving. And praying. And feeling stressed.

And I started to hear the lessons. Not the harsh critical voices I had been accustomed to hearing, the ones that would yell, 'What were you thinking??' and 'Why do you have to be so stubborn??' and 'Why didn't you just stop when you could??'

No, that day's lessons were delivered through the gentle voice of my inner self as the miles kept ticking by and the gas gauge continued to drop..

These gentle thoughts went like this: 'You have limits. Whether you recognize them or not, you will always have limits. You don't have to do everything, nor are you supposed to. You don't have to be a superwoman. You won't please everyone, so stop beating yourself up and take a break when you need to.'

And they continued: 'Or you can keep going and going...but eventually, there will be nothing left, and you may not get to choose how and when you can refuel yourself. Like this car, the farther you try to push yourself without stopping and the longer you go before refueling, the more stress and tension you are going to feel. Until you can go no farther.'

It was a pretty powerful analogy as the gas gauge was now staying in the red. A sign said the next exit was in 11 miles: Pine Bluffs, Wyoming. When I reached that exit, I would be 342 miles from where I had started that morning. I knew I had to get off at that exit, because it would be very unwise and possibly unsafe to go any farther.

Exit 1 on the Wyoming side of I-80 west to Pine Bluffs was a construction exit, but I no longer cared. There was nothing off of that exit. I no longer cared. I pulled off the exit far enough to stop the car and turn it off while I looked around and assessed my surroundings. I didn't even dare let the car idle as I pulled out my phone and prayed for service and tried to figure out how to use my GPS for the first time ever.

I looked at the little town of Pine Bluffs off to the left. (Later, I found out it has a population of a little over 1,000 people.) Surely there would be a gas station there! And please let it be open on a Sunday! My GPS showed one blue dot on the map. I just had to continue off the exit and turn left onto Hwy 30 and then drive two miles into town to find a gas station. I couldn't see it, though; couldn't see anything, really, other than small-town-in-the-middle-of-nowhere Wyoming buildings. I was really wishing I wasn't in this situation, dependent on what I could not see and my questionable GPS skills for something I now desperately needed. But the only thing I could do was either have trust or stay on the side of the road forever. And staying still wouldn't get me fuel.

I almost missed the gas station. There were actually two. Ironically, I had stopped at one with my husband when we had taken a trip across the country the previous November.

I had never felt such gratitude for a gas station attendant before. Or for the very clear instructions from my inner self to 'Get off the interstate now!' When I headed back to the interstate, I saw that the second Pine Bluffs exit that would have led directly to the gas station was closed. I had to follow a detour back down Hwy 30 to reconnect to the interstate.

The travel stop I had been thinking of was another 22 miles past Pine Bluffs. I don't know if I would have made it.

Take what you want from my experience, even if it is just the information that there is no visible place to refuel between Sidney, Nebraska and Pine Bluffs, Wyoming.

The lesson was clear: we all have limits. Sometimes, we know what they are; sometimes, we only think we know what they are; sometimes, we push past them. And sometimes we ignore them. Whatever we choose to do, whether we acknowledge them or not, they are there. My little car had a limit. I thought I knew what it was. But that limit was dependent upon load and wind and hills and speed and was constantly changing. Just like mine is. But I don't have to guess at what my limits are or worry about them too much if I just listen to my inner voice of wisdom. I will always have a choice...until I am pushed past my limits.

As I reached Cheyenne, Wyoming and turned onto Hwy 59 north toward Gillette, there was a little blue sign off the side of the road that warned, 'No fuel for 75 miles.' I checked my odometer. 197 miles. I could go at least another 145 miles before needing gas, I decided. And off I went."

That's a powerful lesson that I still need. As I tell this story, I am reminded that I still have limitations. That I always will. That I would **never** expect any of my vehicles to perform under the circumstances or in the ways I have expected myself to perform.

A good friend once shared with me a question that had changed her own perception of how she treated herself. I pass it on here: "What would someone who loved herself do?"

That same question was a powerful question for me that day. Deep down, I knew that the way I treated myself needed to change, at least in part. And gradually, I have been changing my ways. I know now that I run much better when I am not tossing out parts of myself or ignoring the warning lights that signal I need attention.

I would like to say that I treat my vehicles well, but I suspect that's a matter of perspective. I change the oil regularly and keep an eye on the wear of the tires. I also pay strict attention to the warning lights. That seems like good maintenance to me, and I generally feel safe on the road. But my car frequently needs a car wash that it rarely gets, and it has needed to be cleaned out for the past year. I don't like to clean the car, though, because generally I wind up taking out and not putting back in the very thing I eventually need, like a water bottle or sweatshirt or blanket or book or shoes or sandwich...

I love my car. And I treat it well according to my own needs. I also love myself, and I'm doing my best to treat myself well. Which, much like the way I maintain and care for my car, is specific to me. And may not look at all the way others think it should.

I'm okay with that. If I treat myself the way I treat my car, I'll stay in pretty good shape.

9

Am I Always This Quiet?

In those early years, what I felt most often was frustration. I was defensive, angry, and stirred up, but mainly, I was frustrated. My frustration was what showed up the most in therapy sessions, and it was also the feeling I could least admit to having. I was frustrated by not understanding what was happening. Frustrated that progress was so slow. Frustrated that I couldn't figure out what I was missing to make things improve faster. Frustrated by questions I could not answer and things I felt I could not say.

Did I mention that I often felt frustrated??

One of the most memorable experiences of feeling that frustration happened when I made my first visit to Sedona, Arizona to attend the John Barnes Healing Seminar. While I was going to be there for the seminar, I had also scheduled two treatment sessions at the therapy center. I had bitten my tongue through treatments before and left feeling more angry than I did when I came in, but those two treatments that week pushed me far beyond what I had experienced before.

At the start of one of them, my therapist walked into the room and almost immediately asked, "Are you always this quiet?"

Oh.

There was a small, quiet "yes" from me. And then...shutdown.

You see, one of the things I was most afraid of had just happened: much like the first time I walked into Michael's office, I felt "seen." And that scared me as much as it made me feel angry and defensive.

The session went on from there, and the therapist asked other questions that just made me simmer even more inside. I simmered so much that I eventually left an angry note for my therapist tucked into the door of the clinic when I headed out of town at the end of the seminar.

How *dare* he ask me the questions he did?! What did it matter if I was always that quiet? And how did he know that to begin with?? He had just barely walked into the room!

His question of "Are you always this quiet?" stuck inside me like a thorn for many, many months. It was the kind of question that rattled around inside until I started to examine it. Started to examine my beliefs and behaviors about being and staying quiet. Started to examine what made me feel so angry to be asked that question to begin with.

Early on, I had learned that the questions that stuck around and irritated and annoyed me were simply little beacons of internal light highlighting something that needed to be explored and dug out. I started to look for the belief behind the behavior and eventually found that many of my answers came in dreams, in vague memories of things that may or may not have happened the way I remembered but that my mind formulated a belief and subsequent behavior pattern around.

> *"Years ago, I was asked if I was always so quiet. It is one of those questions that has stuck around and rattled around for a long time now, because as far as I knew, yes, I always have*

been quiet. I assumed it was just my nature. But that hasn't quite rung true.

In 1979, Hurricane Frederic hit the Gulf Coast of Alabama. I was four years old at the time. We spent the night at the church because our house wasn't safe. I look at kids now of a similar age and think of how small I must have been at the time. That seems so little to be tucked under a table (for safety) all alone in a classroom and told to go to sleep, to be quiet, to be 'good.' To not disturb the other families there in the church that night. To not make trouble for my mother, who was taking care of the baby of the family. To not be like my sister, who wouldn't stop crying and had to be taken out of the room. A family friend held her and played with her and fed her crackers in the kitchen while I was told to be quiet and good and to go to sleep. I was so scared. The light was turned off, and I was left alone.

It probably doesn't seem like that event was such a big deal, but it was for me at the time. When I look back at that now, it isn't hard to see how my beliefs formed, the beliefs that my needs were unimportant and that it didn't matter if I was scared or didn't want to be alone. The beliefs that others came first and that the best thing I could do for anyone was to stay hidden and safe and quiet even though I needed otherwise. A lifetime of behaviors were shaped by that one event and were reinforced over and over throughout the years.

That inner child who showed up in a therapy session last week just wanted to be held. That's the me who so frequently ends up under the table and doesn't want to come back out, the me who has been so quiet, the me who hasn't spoken up for what I need...

I didn't know that I needed help processing through the events I have perceived as trauma.

I have so many memories of those early years in Alabama... I have heard that most events that shape our beliefs happen by the age of ten, and we lived in Alabama until I was eight. My brother was born there. At just under a year old, he was the baby in the family when the hurricane hit. My mom almost died having him. I have vague memories of being sent to stay with family friends around that time, separated from my siblings since people couldn't take in all of us. That might have been when my mom was on bedrest before and after my brother's birth...or again when my next sister was born in 1980...or when the next was born in 1983. Those were all hard pregnancies and deliveries for my mom. Again, I was told to be good, be quiet, don't cause trouble. Vague, vague memories of a childhood spent being quiet... I can only imagine the things I might have overheard from the people I stayed with: that my mom might die, that she shouldn't be having another child. I can only imagine the stress my dad must have felt. He was 27 when my brother was born, then 29 when the next (the fifth) child was born. I can only imagine how that affected all of us at the time. I suspect those experiences formed many of my feelings about pregnancy and childbirth, things I wasn't totally aware of even with the births of my own girls. But those feelings were very much there: fear, withdrawal, an inability to feel deep love and desire for those pregnancies, wanting what I was told to want. But mostly fear.

Today is about feeling through my emotions, feeling through the things that originally shaped my beliefs, feeling through the things I missed out on in life because of those beliefs. Not an easy task—I've missed out on a lot. And at the moment, there is a great deal of sadness and anger and blame and then guilt for blaming, because I really can't imagine how hard those years must have been for my parents."

If I were to describe my life to someone, it would never occur to me to talk about traumatic events during my early years. I grew up in a home where I generally felt provided for and safe, in a home with two parents and plenty of siblings. I wasn't abused or neglected or abandoned. I didn't have to get a job at a young age. Didn't have to work for the things I took for granted: a roof over my head, food, clothing. Part of me knows it was a good childhood and that I should feel grateful.

Only my brain did not necessarily perceive life that way. I eventually came to realize that things that had happened long ago and had been buried deep inside were actually pivot points along the way to developing my belief system about life. In this particular instance, that chain of events shaped how I felt about being quiet: quiet equaled good, and I wanted to be considered "good." Being good meant being loved, and all anyone really wants in this life is to be loved. Therefore, I was quiet.

My subconscious connected the dots years ago from those times I was told to be quiet and reinforced that "be quiet" belief as I grew up, as I told myself stories about how the world worked. And I lived with that belief and the behavior it created until I gained enough awareness to dig it out and examine it.

Other beliefs have surfaced from the hurricane.

> *"I remember my dad coming to get me when it was quiet. We walked out of the front doors of the church, and he showed me the trees that had been blown down. He had me listen to the quiet that was the eye of the storm. He told me we were in the middle of the hurricane and that it was coming back...and then he took me back to my place under the table and told me to stay there and go to sleep. I must have at some point, because the next thing I remember is trying to go home in the morning.*

To my four-year-old self, it must have looked like the end of everything. I have seen the pictures as an adult, but I still have memories from a little person's perspective, and I remember that everything looked so big. We couldn't drive home all the way, so we walked along streets with downed trees, downed power poles. Our porch roof was blown off. There was a tree on top of the house. I stepped on a nail in the yard and thought I was going to get lockjaw and die. So many subconscious beliefs formed from this event.

The more I have let whatever needs to come up come up, the more I can see how formative that one night was so many years ago. Perhaps it was the beginning of so many beliefs that have shaped my life and been repeated over and over, or at least those have been the only messages I could hear:

'Be really quiet so that you don't disturb others.'

'The needs of others are more important than yours. Your needs actually aren't important at all.'

'Stay there. Don't move. There is danger if you do.'

'Home is not safe.'

'You will be left alone in the dark when there is something really scary happening.'

'Just go to sleep. There is nothing anyone can do to help you. Nothing anyone is going to do to help you.'

I formed the belief that I didn't matter. Because no one ever came."

Subconscious beliefs can be powerful things, and they must be examined in order to live a healthy life. Not examining them is like leaving your life on autopilot with no understanding of where things are headed or why. You have no sense of control. The direction was determined long before and based on events you may not even fully remember.

Surely, that can't be a good way to live.

The amazing thing about being brave enough and persistent enough to dig out your beliefs is that you can change them. And you also just might find that things don't always mean what you think they mean.

> *Nov 16, 2017*
>
> *"It's sobering to see how hard I've been trying to change who I am. And to realize that not only can I not do that (as much as I've wanted to), there is a part of me that doesn't want to change at all. And maybe it has nothing to do with commitment. Now that I'm seeing the part of me that has been keeping me safe from the change I thought I needed, it's sobering to think how much would have been lost if I had succeeded. Sobering to begin to see how little things have been twisted ever so slightly in my perception. Sobering to realize that for all I thought I have learned, I am also seeking to simply accept myself as I am, feeling it sinking in that maybe I do know exactly who I am. I've just been trying to fix and change who I am rather than simply allowing me to be. It's sobering to realize that I really don't know anything, after all. Perhaps the best thing to do is to stop trying to figure any of it out."*

I could not see it at the time, but a question posed to me long ago became a catalyst to recognizing and embracing something that is an essential part of who I am.

> *"I've written before about the first interaction I ever had with a therapist at Therapy on the Rocks, the one who asked if I*

was always that quiet. I felt so defensive when he asked me that.

I've realized my quietness is a gift. One I've spent so much time thinking was somehow bad, one I used to use to beat myself up, thinking that I needed to talk or participate or join in. I completely missed that quietness is a gift. It allows me to feel with my heart, to hear what isn't said, to listen to and see the hearts of others. Helping heal hearts is what I'm here to do.

Words are totally inadequate.
One of the things I have most disliked about myself—the thing that made me tell myself I'm small and unnoticed—is perhaps one of the greatest gifts I've been given."

It can be quite the feeling to realize one day just how hard you have been trying to change something about yourself...and then to suddenly find yourself feeling grateful that you *didn't* succeed, because if you had, a part of you would be incomplete.

Examine the beliefs. Let the questions be asked. Let the answers come in whatever form they may. And trust what you feel when they do.

Yes, sometimes I am that quiet. And when I am, it is a good thing—it is a part of *me*, after all.

10

What About Giddy?

Like the questions that have stuck and rattled around inside until I examined them, many snippets of advice and observations from others have stuck, too, forming words and phrases that act as reminders when my internal chatter gets loud.

One of those is that you don't have to believe everything you think.

Case in point: giddy.

When my husband tells the story of how we met, he uses the word "giddy." And I don't like it. To me, "giddy" implies a girly, twitter pated silliness. Holding his hand while roller-skating did not make me "giddy"—it was just fun. I was not a giddy, love-struck girl. I did not like that word. Thought it was a useless word that should never be applied to me.

Apparently, I just didn't know what the word actually meant.

According to Merriam-Webster, giddy is an adjective that has two meanings. First and foremost, it means "being dizzy," as in "being giddy" from doing unaccustomed exercise. Or it can mean something that causes dizziness, as in saying that a height is a "giddy height" or that being on a rapidly-whirling merry-go-round causes one "to feel giddy."

I have actually spent much of the last several years feeling giddy and just didn't know it. I just knew I hated much of it: the dizziness I got upon standing or turning my head and waiting for my sense of balance to catch up, the dizziness I got when I moved too fast (as in faster than a turtle moving through peanut butter), when my body was tense and tight and my brain was overwhelmed by additional movement. Instant dizziness.

Yet I have purposely induced other moments of dizziness: at the park, on all manner of contraptions that spin and twirl; in chairs and on rollercoasters and on merry-go-rounds. I love the sensation of spinning around and around! Of closing my eyes and feeling the spinning sensations throughout my body...

...Which seems weird considering how much I hate being dizzy.

I apparently only hate it when I can't control it or make it stop, or when I've been caught completely off-guard. There have been moments during therapy sessions where it suddenly felt like the table tilted and I was slowly sliding off of it, or when my eyes were closed and I felt the room start to spin. There were several days when I would take the elevator up to the third floor of the office building where I worked and feel the dizziness build inside with the starting and stopping motion. I would step off and feel the hallway tip to the right under my feet, feel the accompanying nausea and disorientation, get to the office and feel the world tilt away from me. I'd be totally caught by surprise and unsure if the feeling would pass before my first client of the day showed up.

I have had a love/hate relationship with giddiness and didn't even know it.

The big surprise came recently, when I felt ridiculously happy after my pelvis adjusted and a friend commented that I was giddy. In considering whether or not that was an accurate statement, I learned the second meaning of the word, which actually is somewhat related to the meaning my husband was using years ago. The second definition of "giddy," according to Merriam-Webster, is being lightheartedly silly, frivolous, joyfully elated, or euphoric. (My husband may have been correct after all! Because I *was* feeling lightheartedly silly when I was holding his hand and roller-skating...)

What does any of this have to do with not believing everything I think?

John Barnes teaches about the importance of the pelvis being balanced. When it is not—when there are misalignments in the pelvic bones—structurally, that can create the appearance and bodily perception of having a long and short leg. Every time the body takes a step, that long-and-short-leg scenario creates an imbalance in walking. The brain and central nervous system perceive danger in this, namely an inherent instability, a sense of falling off a curb with every step. This can create a deep sense of fear and anxiety in the body until the pelvis is balanced and aligned and a stable foundation is created.

Intellectually, I've known this—when I first heard John Barnes teach this concept years ago, it resonated with me as truth. But the experience of feeling the difference between a balanced and unbalanced pelvis is far beyond what I expected.

I've been aware of my fear of movement for a while now, been aware that I brace in my lower back when I bend down, that I feel the need to move slowly and have support. I feel the fear in my body when I do not, when I am startled and bend or move quickly without being prepared to do so. While attending a movement workshop, I became even more aware of this internal fear—squatting and hinging from my hips made me move hesitantly, with braced, slow movements. It seems like standing a few feet away from a wall and reaching back with the hips to touch the wall should be easy, but for me, it wasn't. I had a great deal of difficulty trying to do this. My knees would bend and I would lean forward, yes, but reaching back with my hips was scary, and I would get off-balance and fall. I didn't want to bend.

My pelvis has been tilted and rotated for a long time. My pubic symphysis has been sheared for a long time. I didn't know just how much that had been contributing to my internal fear and bracing and anxiety until last night, when my pubic symphysis adjusted. For the first time ever. *Ever*. Hallelujah!

The immediate change in my internal environment is not one I could ever adequately describe. I sat up and noticed that I was sitting differently. I stood, and I was standing differently. I felt ridiculously happy. You couldn't have wiped the grin from my face. Something deep inside knew, without even taking a step, *knew* that I could do a deep squat.

And I did. Right there. No wall. No support. No hesitation. No fear. Easy.

I did it again. And then again.

My smile just kept getting bigger.

Easy.

I had no idea just how much my pelvic imbalances were contributing to my internal fear and bracing. I just thought I couldn't do the movements. On the bad days, I wondered if I was reaching for too much or hoping for more than I was really meant to have. A part of me kept trying to convince me that it was enough to not hurt all the time, enough to just be able to work and enjoy life. "Stop trying to do more!" I heard.

And then there was the part of me that knew that couldn't be true. So I kept working on hip mobility and restoring pliability and mobility to my body's stuck issues and tissues. I kept showing up to treatment sessions and the training sessions and pushing through the healing crises I occasionally would slam into.

I didn't realize the missing piece was my pelvic alignment until it literally clicked back into place.

And I felt giddy.

I've often heard that our greatest strength is also our greatest weakness. In this case, one of the things I've fought with and struggled with the most—dizziness—is expressed by a word that also means "joy" and "lightheartedness." The very things I have been searching for.

Not a coincidence.

Today, the word "giddy" is a reminder to embrace the parts of me that I hate, the parts of me that I think are bad, the parts of me that I am trying so desperately to fix or change. They are a part of me. Trying to get rid of them is struggling and fighting with myself. Even if I win that fight, a part of me still loses, and that is counterproductive to everything I have been trying to do: find me, find wholeness, find integrity. I cannot do any of those things if I am fighting with myself.

And so I embrace both meanings of "giddy." I still experience both meanings. Obviously, I like one experience more than the other, but they are both part of me.

Good thing I don't always believe what I think.

11

Have I Been Small Long Enough?

Another recurring theme throughout my journey has been the belief that I am small. Insignificant. That my needs don't matter. That no one will hear me even if I do speak up, so don't bother. "Small" often goes with "quiet."

Plenty of motivational speakers talk about playing the role of "small" in our lives and how that affects us. How it is not who we are or who we are meant to be.

I *have* felt bits and pieces of me grow and expand inside, but there has often been a holding back along with that expansion. In describing this to Michael once, he asked just how big was I? At the time, I didn't know.

Until one day, I did.

> *May 26, 2018*
>
> *"Sometimes, it feels like my system reboots. A glitch happens, a bad day, a coming to a slow and grinding halt that ends in a crash. My world slowly tilts and dumps me in a messy heap into that hole I have hated.*
>
> *When that happens, I spend some time there, letting myself feel the tears and anger and frustration, feeling through it.*

I've learned that if I don't stop when I feel the warning signs, the crash still comes—I can't avoid it. Putting it off only intensifies it, and it tends to catch me by surprise when it can no longer be contained. Better to just stop for a bit before it becomes overwhelming and I melt down somewhere even more inconvenient and messy.

I've learned that I will keep coming out on the other side. At least the fear that I won't isn't still stopping me... I've learned that allowing myself time to be in those places when I need to be there helps me feel a bit better: a bit less weighed down, like I have a clean slate again.

But I keep coming back to the same patterns afterward, the same habits of behavior and thought. That clean slate gets filled with the same things that filled it before. Until I come to that glitch again. And crash again, feeling twisted and compressed and small inside. Thinking that the thing is what's causing the problem...and not realizing that I am the thing. So frustrated...

This time, someone is there to help me change the pattern.

'Go in to find the answers,' he says.

'Feel the compression.

Feel the twist.

Feel the tightness.

Get smaller.

And tighter.

Until that is all you feel.

And then even smaller.'

I can't breathe! There's no room left.

'Even smaller,' he says.

'Feel the space there. Find a home there. You are the thing.'

I don't understand. I don't want to understand. I don't want to stay in that space that is so cramped and small and tight.

'Come back to the stillness,' he says. 'Be in the stillness.'

But what is this space? This is the place I often fight so hard to get out of. I need to move! I don't want to be in this space!

I feel its smallness...and stay anyway.

What is this space????

I get so small and compressed and twisted and there is nowhere else to go. Nothing else to feel.

So still... There is nothing else to do but feel and be.

Accepting what is. Admitting what is.

I am the thing.

I feel like a twisted and compressed and small lump of coal.

I am twisted and compressed and small.

I feel my beliefs about that and what I have wanted to be instead. It's the beliefs that are causing the problems...

'Move from there,' he says.

I have been so small and so compressed for so long that I can't feel my legs. Moving from that space, I can't feel from my waist down.

I wait.

Never before have I experienced the intensity of a sensation like that coming into the entirety of both of my legs. Throughout my entire legs. Nothing to do but stay with it. Can't move until I sink all the way back in. Even then, it is difficult to stand.

Why is it so difficult to stand?? What am I trying to keep from being seen?

I stand.

I can't feel the ground...can't find the ground.

'Connect your legs to the ground,' he says.

I can't find it. There's too much in between. We're on the third floor. Too much space.

'You're still thinking small,' he says.

I want to jump and stomp and smash through those layers. I can feel those shell-like layers between me and the earth.

I'll feel silly doing it. Really silly.

I do it anyway.

It's 6 p.m. on a holiday weekend. Who knows who is still working on the floor beneath us?

I don't really care... I'm doing it anyway. Silly or not, I start to stomp and jump.

And now I'm mad. Stupid floor. Stu. Pid. Floor! I can't get through. Still can't find the ground. I stomp and stomp and stomp. And am still not connected.

And now I know why my legs hurt so much.

I pause. Out of breath. Tired of trying. Stupid floor.

'Feel your legs,' he says. 'Feel them connect...all...the...way...down...to ...the...ground...'

WHAM! I feel the impact like a thunderbolt go through my sacrum, through my legs, through the floor, deep into the earth.

And instantly, I'm connected. With a magnetic sensation of energy flowing up from the earth through my legs and whole body.

Wow.

Didn't know that was possible.

I expand from there. I find my home.

'You never left,' he says.

I feel the truth of that in a way I haven't before.

'Who are you?' he asks.

Words are insufficient for what I have seen and felt. But I know. I feel the answer. I see the answer. In that moment, I know who I am more than I have ever known.

It most likely won't change a bit about this thing I call life. Except how I approach it. Which changes everything...

I'm still human. Will most likely still have good days and bad days and ups and downs and everything in between. The perspective and the need to fight those has changed, though. Again.

I have found that this is my process of life. It is in the very things I have been writing about and drawing about for several years now. It is in those moments of needing to wander off for some time alone to regroup and vent and cry and throw a tantrum. Those moments I have labeled as being depression or falling apart or having a meltdown and tried to avoid because I considered them to be bad moments. But now I'm beginning to see them for the pattern they are. The slowing down and becoming very still and growing colder and colder as I feel into the very things I hate is my process of life and transformation.

It's like entering a cocoon and being reborn each time. Shedding another layer of something each time."

I try really hard to remember these moments...only somehow life happens, and I don't. And somehow I keep coming back to this lesson. I'm wondering if perhaps feeling small is like feeling quiet. Maybe there is something I don't yet understand about it.

I'm still waiting for that next layer of understanding and integration.

Maybe I haven't felt small long enough yet.

I suspect, though, that I just haven't realized I have had permission all along to get as big as I want. Even as I write this book, that realization is sinking in. I've needed the space and permission to stay small. Needed it to work through things, feel through things.

It has only been recently that I realized I don't need to stay small anymore. At least, I don't right now. That space will be there when and if I need it again.

It is only after feeling small for long enough that I am finding just how big I am. This is a completely different type of feeling, one I will be exploring for quite a while.

I guess I've answered that question for myself, after all.

How about you? Have you been small long enough?

12

The Thing I Couldn't Admit to Anyone

I talked earlier about setbacks: the times when I felt worse before things got better, the times I forgot what I had learned and had to be reminded of them. There have been some difficult times during this journey, to be sure, but I call them "setbacks" for a reason, "ups and downs" for a reason. No matter how bad things got, some part of me still knew I was making progress and that the setback was temporary.

Until, that is, the week I hit rock-bottom. I hit what I felt was the end. It happened about 2 ½ years into my journey. By then, I was a myofascial release therapist myself; I had attended almost 150 hours of training with John Barnes and his staff and felt like I had a pretty good understanding of the healing process.

But I found there was more to go. Deeper to go. Time to admit something I never thought I would admit to anyone. To face what I had been avoiding for so long. To sit with something that literally felt like it was going to kill me.

> *September 19, 2016*
>
> *"This entry takes more than a usual amount of courage to write. As I write it, I worry what others will think more than I usually do. I don't want others to worry; I don't want to be looked at funny; I don't want to scare my family. Because I*

am okay, I really am—there are just some things I need to say in the interest of my own soul-clearing.

I have been battling what I call demons inside for a long time. Someone who has become a dear friend asked me a few years ago if I was depressed. I absolutely refused to consider the possibility. I was mentally closed that day to any further discussion. Refused to admit what I might be struggling with. Depression isn't supposed to happen to people with pretty good lives who don't have any apparent problems or out-of-the-ordinary challenges. Isn't supposed to happen to people just doing their best to be good.

Only...it does. And that day, my friend could see something that I couldn't.

We talk of staying focused on the positive, on seeing the good. I wrote about that recently. But throughout all of my attempts to stay positive, I was constantly pushing down and trying to ignore the voices that were telling me otherwise: 'You're not good enough.' 'You will never get it right.' 'Give up.' 'You're not worth the effort.'

If I could stay busy enough, they weren't as loud. If I could do things well enough, I could tell myself what the voices said wasn't true. If I could set and accomplish really hard goals, I could tell myself I had done something worthwhile, that my life had as much meaning as possible. If I could just be spiritual enough, maybe the voices would disappear.

Kept doing my absolute best to avoid those demons. Refusing to admit they were there; believing that if I did, that would somehow mean they had won.

But sometimes, avoiding things only makes them that much

more determined to find a way to get your attention; sometimes, avoiding them only makes them yell louder.

The demons I have hoped and hoped and hoped were not a part of me finally appeared in a way that I could no longer ignore. I could no longer pretend they didn't exist, because they showed themselves with all the voices of belief that I have about demons and evil. They appeared with threats of making my life a living hell, of wreaking havoc and destruction on all that I think is good about myself. Of swallowing me slowly in the darkness and laughing with spite as they did.

I am not the person I have tried to convince myself I am.

I've known the demons were there. Not by name, no, but no matter how much I tried to ignore and avoid them, I felt a...something... I was deeply afraid of the something that was lurking there, just below the surface.

I knew I couldn't get rid of them, that I couldn't banish them. But I tried to. And the demons laughed as they rose and clung to my skull by the tips of their fingers, tormenting and taunting me. I knew they didn't want token acceptance, either—they could feel the falsehood in my intent when I tried to give them that.

I got to the point where I wondered if anyone could even help me anymore, to the point where I considered walking away and maybe not coming back. I wondered—if I walked far enough, would the voices in my head get tired and quit talking? Would the demons that were following me stop somewhere else along the way?

I felt like I was literally in hell. A faceless, nameless hell where my existence was absolutely worthless...except maybe to my family, who have needs I couldn't meet because I couldn't even meet my own. Which is its own version of hell.

I don't know if that is depression or not. I do know that I started to contemplate suicide. That wasn't something new, though—suicide is one of the demons that has been following me around for a long time. I had just never felt its presence as strongly.

Years ago, I had gone through the experience of someone close to me leaving a note that she was going somewhere to kill herself. I remember what it did to those of us who knew her. I said that would never happen to me—I would never do that, I thought. I didn't understand how life could seem so bad that someone would ever consider doing that. I know now that it isn't necessarily about life being bad or overwhelming as much as it maybe is about the voices and demons inside loudly insisting that life is bad or overwhelming and that you are worthless and life is pointless.

My fear of those demons was big, so big. I believed that if I ever admitted that I sometimes really wondered if my life was worthless that it would somehow become so. I could hear the beliefs, and I could tell myself they were lies. But that fear was powerful. Whatever that thing was that I was trying to hide from was powerful. And I just knew that when it came out, someone was going to get hurt, either me or someone else. And I knew that I wouldn't be able to fix it—when that happened, I wouldn't be save-able ever again. Not then, and not in the ultimate scheme of things. I found out I apparently didn't believe in repentance and forgiveness, at least not for me. The voices convinced me that was true. And as long as I didn't mess up too much, I just might have a chance of getting to heaven. A part of me absolutely knew, though, that I would never have that chance once whatever was inside got out. And

I knew that if I ever got to the point where I believed that, then life would be pointless, hopeless. No longer worth living.

The day those demons came out, I spent a very long time walking and deciding on how and where I would go to kill myself. The demons followed me like dust follows Pigpen in the Peanuts movie. Eventually, I realized I would never be able to walk farther than the demons and voices inside that were slowly killing me. I felt lost and confused and hurt and very scared inside. Like something was garbled and tangled and I couldn't even communicate with myself, like something had taken over that was far beyond my comprehension. I felt like I was not in any way who I thought I was, that I wasn't in control of anything inside anymore.

Another dear friend told me that until I stopped and faced what I was most afraid of inside, I would be a runaway. Nothing but a runaway. That I would expend every bit of energy I had for the rest of my life running from what I thought was there.

She was right.

That day, I was told that it seemed like I was at a crossroads: I could let the demons keep chasing me, or I could turn and face them. I was told that if I was willing and ready to face them, there was help. I was reminded to trust that I am worth saving.

I think maybe I came to terms with myself during all the walking I did that day. I decided I would not die that day. That little suicide demon... I think I eventually picked him up and carried him under my arm because he got tired and I felt sorry for him.

There are people who cross our paths when we need them. People who hear and see things we cannot see ourselves. People who say things we could not have thought of ourselves and are maybe completely unaware of the impact of what they've said. I feel like I have walked through hell and survived, in part because of those people. Demons and voices may always be a part of me, but I think maybe I can accept that because I have faced them. I know I don't have to believe everything I think. Avoiding the demons and pretending they weren't there didn't work—it only allowed things to build until they almost consumed me.

Steven Curtis Chapman has a song he calls 'Take Another Step.' In the lyrics, he says, 'We walk by faith and not by sight. We know it's true. We say it and sing it and love the way it sounds. But none of us can even begin to truly understand what it really means until all the lights go out. And there we are. Nothing to hold on to. But the promises God's made to me and you. Take another step.'

I have been there. This is me, taking another step.

I write for me. I write so I will remember. I write in an attempt to be honest with myself. My husband says to share."

Rock-bottom for me was the day I admitted I didn't know if I wanted to continue living or not. When I admitted I was considering suicide. When I felt like if I held still for just a moment longer, I would die. When I felt like I could sit on a rock at the edge of the road and simply decide to stop breathing. And that it would be okay.

Unexamined, ignored, and avoided things weighed on me until I hit rock-bottom. And I stayed there until I allowed myself to fully feel through them. Only then could I move on.

It was another pivot point.

Hitting-rock bottom truly gives you only one direction to take. I stayed there for a while; I've revisited it more than once. And have continued to get back up.

13

What Do I Feel When I Unclench?

Words mean things. And often, it is the smallest subtlety in a phrase that makes the difference. For example, "What do you feel when you unclench?" This question unlocked a whole Pandora's box of feeling when I was asked it one day during a session. I was stuck, my body clenched with tension. A familiar pattern of strain was running through my neck and shoulders and lower back. I was clenched tight, afraid to move.

Michael didn't ask, "What *will* you feel *if* you unclench?" That would have tossed me into intellectual thinking and gotten me stuck even deeper in thinking and trying to figure things out.

Instead, he asked, "What *do* you feel *when* you unclench?"

Rather than my brain thinking harder, my body heard and answered. Mentally and physically, the response inside was, "Huh, I don't know... What *do* I feel?"

I had to unclench in order to find out.

It was like magic to feel my body answering as some of those tight, braced areas unclenched and I started to feel into the things the clenching had been protecting. It was almost irrelevant to me that I immediately felt pain in my lower back. Irrelevant to feel pain in my neck that reached up into my head and behind my eyes.

My body knew how to unclench! I did not know I had that power. Not really. Not to that extent.

I've come back to that question frequently when I get stuck and feel my body twisting into tighter and tighter knots inside. When I have the awareness of what is going on, I remember to ask that question. And instead of thinking about it, I ask the question and then let my body respond.

It especially helps at night. Again, maybe it is just me, but often by the time I get to bed, I have worked a long day and my body is tired. My shoulders might be aching or my back might be a little tight. I lie down, hoping to feel my body relax as I start to drift off to sleep. It doesn't often happen that way, though—for whatever reason, when I am most tired is when my body is also often the most tight. Trying to relax so I can go to sleep simply frustrates me and makes things tighter inside.

Being able to ask a question, though, that my body can hear and answer... Well, that still never ceases to amaze me. It really is like magic.

Why does that matter?

Because one of the major areas of difficulty comes when we numb out, when we tune out and clench tightly and brace and forget that we are tight and braced.

And it still happens to me.

I can be standing and doing something like washing the dishes or working on the countertop with my arms extended in front of me, and I'll start to feel a dull pain in the base of my skull or a gnawing tension behind my eyes.

For just a brief second, I wonder why I am getting a headache. Even now, subtle patterns can initially show themselves. Did I do too much? Did I not get enough sleep? Am I standing wrong?

And then I remember to check in with my body. When I do, nine times out of ten, I find that I am clenching somewhere, usually through my lower back and pelvic floor. And that tension is being distributed throughout my body and eventually ends up pulling on my head.

What do I feel when I unclench? Usually tiredness. Perhaps exasperation to be doing a chore I don't want to be doing or feel I shouldn't be doing because someone *else* made the mess. These thoughts and feelings start to cause tension in my body. But once recognized, I can breathe, consider if there is another way to go about what I am doing, make a choice, unclench, and aaahhh... No more headache.

It's not the posture—it's the clenching that is holding the posture in place. It's the inner dialogue and story I am telling myself that are causing the bracing. Change the story, examine the beliefs, choose to unclench, allow my body to soften, and the posture changes and the headache is relieved.

I recently heard someone ask what advice one might give his or her younger self. It wasn't a question directed at me, but I had a ten-hour drive home afterward to consider it for myself.

What would I say to a younger me?

Granted, the lessons I have learned from my experiences are what have shaped me into the person I have become, and I wouldn't want to necessarily change that. But if I could go back and give myself one piece of advice, it would be this:

"It's okay to feel. Life is going to throw a lot of crappy stuff at you, and you are going to want to clench and brace and harden against it. You can absolutely choose to do that. Sometimes, it might seem necessary to do that in order to survive. But as often as you can, allow yourself to feel life rather than clench against it. It's okay to feel heartache, loss, grief, suffering, pain, and anguish. It's okay to feel anger, jealousy, resentfulness, meanness, and pettiness. It's also okay to feel joy, love, peace, wonder, amazement, and amusement. Allow yourself to feel it all."

In the beginning months of healing, I made a list of all of the emotions I thought I was familiar with through personal experience. Within that list, 72 of them fell into a negative category and 3 of them were positive. I then made a list of the emotions I would like to feel and experience. That list had 15 positive emotions on it that I thought I had never experienced (or had forgotten what they felt like), emotions like "outgoing," "elated," "secure," "light-hearted," and "lovable."

Looking back, I have to wonder if I truly had never experienced them or if I had just not recognized them for what they were at the time.

Regardless, most of us do not hold on to the positive emotions and dwell on them. We don't lock joy deep inside and worry about what others think of us for feeling joyful. We don't hide them and hope that nobody will see or comment on how we are feeling. We don't judge ourselves for feeling that way—rather, we often freely share the good things we feel.

It is the negative things that get stuck, the negative things we hold on to and use to beat ourselves up. The negative things are what we try most to hide or what we clench and brace against because they seem so painful and overwhelming.

But the only way to fully heal is to let go of those things, to unclench and allow ourselves to feel through them rather than hold on to them.

To my younger self, I would say: it is okay to feel. It is okay to feel *all* that life will bring.

To my self now, I gently ask: what do you feel when you unclench?

To you, I ask the same: what are you holding on to so tightly? Why? Is it really worth the energy and effort? What do YOU feel when you unclench?

14

Have I Learned From the Times I Messed Up?

This one has been a doozy of a question for me. I have learned lots of things from the times I messed up, like learning to hide or lie or shove things under the rug so nobody would know about them. I've learned to let others go first so that I am not the first to mess up—with any luck, I won't mess up if they do it right and I can copy what they did closely enough. I've learned to pretend and fake my way through. I've learned to not care about things I couldn't fake my way through. And I've eventually learned to not want to try at all because of fear I would fail.

Yes, I did learn from the times I messed up. I learned to not want, to not hope, to not dream, to not dare.

I've had to revisit and revise all of those lessons. Deeper healing could not happen until I did that.

One lesson in particular came flooding back in horrific detail one night as I revisited a time I thought I had messed up the worst of all.

November 30, 2016

"My second daughter was born by C-section. It wasn't planned and it wasn't an emergency—she just didn't turn like

she should have. She was comfortable there inside with her head tucked up under my ribs. I didn't know until the 39th week that her head was the little round bump I liked feeling. I rubbed it a lot while she was in the womb.

I have mostly come to terms with that C-section and its consequences. I say 'mostly' because I keep finding layers of buried emotion and belief.

It took a long time to acknowledge and admit the anger I didn't know I was holding on to. Anger toward myself and my body for somehow failing to perform correctly. Anger toward my daughter for not being where she was supposed to be (and accompanying guilt because that couldn't possibly have been her fault). Anger toward the doctor for not discovering her position until my last regular scheduled visit before my expected delivery. How could he not have known?!

A lot of buried anger that has taken a while to work through.

I thought that was all there was.

It wasn't.

There is a phrase that gets stuck in my head sometimes, a message that plays subconsciously over and over: 'I am afraid to move.'

As I tune in to what my body is feeling right now, I hear that message. And I remember that C-section. Remember how afraid to move I was, afraid to move because I might bleed all over. Afraid to move because it might set off a spasm of severe pain. I remember holding deathly still during the epidural so they wouldn't miss, afraid of winding up paralyzed or with nerve damage if I moved. Trying to not even breathe. Then afraid to move because there was an epidural in my back and

I could feel it leaking when I did move. I was scared to death that I would cause damage to my spinal cord if I moved because I didn't know what that fluid was. Afraid to move because I might have torn my stitches.

'Afraid to move.' The phrase is stuck deep inside, playing over and over like a broken record, followed almost always by an 'I can't...' Frozen and paralyzed because I am afraid to move.

There is enough in the realization of that subconscious message to keep me busy for a while.

I was surprised to find more.

There is a story I have never told anyone about my time in the hospital after that C-section. It doesn't even have a bad ending, just a lot guilt and shame.

It's time to let it go.

I remember feeling so tired. They would bring my daughter in when she needed to be nursed, and I would struggle to stay awake. So tired. I would be awakened in the middle of the night and I would turn on a light and make myself sit up so I would stay awake even as I was willing her to hurry and feeling guilty for feeling so selfish.

One time when she finished nursing, I was supposed to put her back in the bassinet. Only I couldn't—I didn't have the energy. It hurt more than I could bear to twist and lift her even that little bit over the edge of the bed and into the bassinet, and I was just so tired. So I laid there holding her for a few minutes until I could make myself move.

And I fell asleep.

I remember waking up and wondering why the light was on…and then I remembered with a jolt what I had been doing. But I wasn't holding my daughter anymore, and I knew I hadn't put her back.

I was hit by a panic I cannot adequately describe when I realized that I did not know where she was…and then I found her between me and the edge of the bed. When I had fallen asleep, she had slipped down beside me.

I could have killed her. I felt so many things in what must have been just a few seconds. She was so small, all swaddled up and helpless. She could have suffocated so easily if I had shifted or if she had slid down beside me differently. I could have killed my child because I was thinking only of myself—I was lazy and selfish and not wanting to move because I hurt, because I was too tired. I was not fit to be a mother. I don't remember how, but I know I immediately put her back in her bassinet. I have never told anyone what happened until now.

I was scared and ashamed and sick with guilt, and I was setting myself up for years of subconscious messages.

This is partially a cautionary tale about the importance of not keeping infants in bed with you.

It is also a cautionary tale of not keeping feelings and emotions buried inside with you.

Those things get trapped there along with whatever you were telling yourself at the time. Trapped and twisted and solidified into messages that seem true about who you are. Buried emotions and subconscious messages control your life without you even knowing it, and until you face them and let them out, they will keep running and quite possibly ruining (or at least making extremely miserable) your life.

I am seeing those messages now, connecting the dots between the things I am struggling with now and my feelings and beliefs then. That was almost 16 years ago.

It's time to let myself soften and change the messages."

The biggest "mess-up" in this case was not falling asleep—it was stuffing down my emotions and believing the stories I created inside about the type of person I am.

Since revisiting this memory, I have learned to be more kind to myself when I think I am messing up. I have read blog posts and books about failing forward, about how we should fail as quickly as possible and as frequently as possible because that is how we learn.

I have gotten a lot of practice at failing forward as I've stopped believing I am small and insignificant, as I have learned to start to speak up and ask and admit there are things I don't know. Sometimes saying "I don't know" feels very much like failure. Not knowing can feel like a lack of something on my part, like I'm somehow messing up.

I am learning that sometimes saying "I don't know" just means I don't actually know.

And that's okay.

15

So Who Am I Really?

For a long time, I expected my myofascial release therapists to fix me. I thought that was their job, what I paid them for. If I could (and I often couldn't), I would tell them what was hurting, and they would address that and I would feel better.

Big lack of understanding on my part.

I have heard more than once during a therapy session that we were "waiting for me." That *I* am the one I seek. I am still learning what that means, but I am starting to learn.

First and foremost, it means I am responsible for my own healing. It is *my* job to find my way. Others may point; others may offer suggestions, questions, directions. But it is *my* footsteps that will take me in one direction or another.

I didn't want that responsibility. Had spent my life playing things safe, letting others be in charge, letting others be responsible. I did that when I chose a spouse or a job or a place to live. I was looking for safety, looking for someone to tell me what to do.

Often, I was looking for someone to blame. Someone other than myself.

I have been waiting for the part of me that knows differently to show up.

I wondered aloud in a session once where was that part of me? Wondered why I felt left alone even amidst the voices in my head yelling loudly about all the things I should be doing and telling me all the ways I was messing up. I often identify with my thoughts and think they are true.

My brain and my thinking intelligence has been in charge for a long time...only, I am not my thoughts. No matter how much I think I am.

I wondered aloud that day where the real commander-in-chief was inside. Where was the leader of my pack?

As I explored that inside, I heard the following conversation between me and my inner self:

> *"She is not absent."*
>
> *"Well, if she is not absent, why is she not leading?!"*
>
> *"Oh, she is."*
>
> *"Well, if she is leading, why is no one following?"*
>
> *"Oh, she will not force. She will wait for me to choose."*

I realized I am looking for a strong, confident leader. Someone who sees and understands and loves. Someone who wants what is best for me. She has been absent for so long, unnoticed for so long, that I do not see that she is the one in charge. . . yet.

Michael helped me understand this further. Leaders—good leaders, that is—do not dictate. They are a focal point. They inspire. They give purpose and then assign the parts to the ones who best fill them. They have the best interests of all at heart.

The only way to allow my inner allegiance to swerve away from listening to the monkey brain I often have inside and toward the deeper, intuitive, wise leader who is also there is to feel.

I have to switch from *thinking* to *feeling*.

I've been aware of how clenched and tightly held I often feel inside. I have been aware of how often that has been a response to thinking and trying so hard to figure things out. It tangles me up in knots until I become incapable of making a decision about anything. This happens because I have let my thoughts be in charge, and they are not meant to be. A part of me is waiting for the leader of my pack, and the leader of my pack is waiting for *me* to trust and follow.

It is *me* I have been waiting for.

I am not the characters in my story. Not the heroine. Not the villain. Not the temptress. Not the whiny child. Not the victim. Not the unsuspecting fool.

I am the *author* of my story.

Everything that has happened to me, everything that does happen to me, everything I have thought I am...it is all part of my story.

There are so many things I have discovered about myself! Things long buried that I had thought were no longer part of my nature. Other things that I have disliked intensely and have tried and tried and tried to change.

Much of my struggle has been spent fighting against myself because I couldn't see that it is all a part of me. Every bit of it is needed.

Michael once told me to stop trying to change how I feel and to instead admit how I feel. The first time I ever did a week of intensive therapy with multiple sessions a day, I started to understand a bit more what he meant.

March 27, 2015

"I am braver than I ever thought I was. But I only know this now because I have felt so scared so many times. Felt the fear pounding in my chest. Felt the voices in my head frantically yelling warnings and listening to them. But today, I can step back and watch and know that I am braver than I ever thought I was. There is a fire-breathing dragon inside just waiting for me to step aside far enough so that he can burn those fears to the ground. It is pretty cool to watch! Amazing what my self and that dragon can do if I let them.

I am stronger than I ever thought I was. But I only know this now because I have felt so small and insignificant and weak in the past, completely incapable of doing anything. I had given up on me; I was hiding in avoidance, falling and failing over and over until I was convinced I could not get back up. But I found out I can. And not only can I get back up, I can stand up and feel my power. I am stronger than I ever knew.

I know now what trust feels like, and now I know I can trust my self in a way I never thought possible. But I only know that because I have lived with the doubt until I thought it was true. Let the voices convince me that I didn't know what I knew. Let habit dictate what I did and how I responded. Forgot that my inner self is impeccable in her wisdom and that I can trust her completely. I know that today: I know have a self I can trust without hesitation

I know I am a work in progress, and me and my self are absolutely okay with this—in fact, we welcome it. It takes a lot of pressure off! Literally. There are so many others who are further along in this journey who show me that it just keeps getting better. That the light inside just keeps getting brighter. That there is so much to enjoy along the way if I just look. And this realization is so different from the rush I have felt to reach a destination just so that I can say 'I have arrived and I am done.' I am a work in progress, and I will quite possibly never be done. And that is a happy thought.

My body wants to move. It actually likes to move! My self knows this, and it wants me to feel and be aware of every bit of it. I only know this now because I have been so stuck in pain. So determined to numb and freeze and bury and not feel. But my self knows that I have an amazing body, so much better than the ones I see in magazines. This self's body is a gift that moves and talks to me and knows how to heal and take care of its self. Amazing! I just hadn't been listening. I am now.

I accepted my self today. Claimed me for me. Dug out gunk and black grime that had been clinging inside. Dug as far as I could. That gunk is no longer welcome. I belong to me. This body is mine. And I accept all of it, even the parts that hurt. Even the parts that have been hurt. Even the parts that still have gunk.

I have a voice. Maybe a few, actually. I thought I didn't. Didn't know how to have a voice or what that meant. But my self has known better.

My self has emotions that don't need to be stuffed down or judged. My self is really good at not judging. It is what I have thought was me that was getting in the way. I like my self's natural expression better than anything I have been consciously trying to do.

I love me. It no longer causes instant resistance to say those words. In fact, it causes no resistance at all. Just a smile and a breath of love for me.

In the words of my therapist, yes, I have been waiting for me. I just didn't understand. Today, though, I am home. And that is a celebration."

More pieces came as I continued to be more honest with myself about how I really felt about my self. As I examined where those beliefs came from and whether or not they were really true. The parts I have thought were bad. The ones I wished were not there. The things I wanted most to change.

Healing has come as I have learned to not only accept those parts of myself, but more importantly, to embrace and love those parts of myself.

"I learn in pictures—I see things inside that teach me or frighten me or both. I have collected an assortment of personalities inside over the last few years, seen them in vivid detail. That may sound strange. But to me, it seemed perfectly natural to see a gremlin hiding behind my right shoulder blade one day. He was the first. He has gradually been joined by a fire-breathing dragon, a sneaky and mischievous imp, an absolutely calm and powerful voice of wisdom, a perky and annoying cheerleader, a little girl standing against a wall yelling, an older girl hidden in the shadows and protected by a silent black panther, and yet another girl sitting with her knees pulled up and her head down in a corner that looks a lot like a prison.

It's a party inside sometimes.

I once polled some of these personalities when I was really struggling with something. The imp had a lot of sarcastic remarks on the subject. The cheerleader insisted in her perky little voice that I could do it. (That just annoyed me.) The little girl in the corner, though, was absolutely silent. She was waiting to be rescued by someone and couldn't help anyone else until she was. The dragon wanted to burn everything down. And the voice of wisdom was noticeably absent.

I see and hear them in great detail.

I have also thought that, other than the voice of wisdom (which I absolutely trust), most of these things are things that do not belong in me. Things I do not want. That I do not like. I was seeing them only in terms of their undesirable characteristics.

That imp is impossibly mischievous. Think of the most sneaky, teasing sort of person you have ever known, someone who gets into everything, who doesn't have respect for rules or boundaries. That person is always into something and has an impish grin and laugh, playing and teasing and then disappearing in an instant. The imp stood at the bottom of a large dam inside one day and painted bright pictures and words in his best blue-graffiti-like style, laughing at my distress as he drew. Didn't care a bit about anything other than the fun he was having.

That impish nature has always tended to get me in trouble.

The others? Cheerleaders in general annoy me. Perky. Bright. Insisting you can do something. Cheerful by definition: 'Yay, team!'

Annoying.

The dragon. Big. Powerful. Slightly scary and intimidating. I watched him burn everything to the ground once. There is no predicting when that might happen. He often appears with no warning, silent and powerful and deadly.

The gremlin built a stash of black and ugly things inside. Hoarded and collected and hid things behind my shoulder blade. All the things I didn't want to look at: anger, greed, hate, jealousy, resentment. Those were the ones I thought I knew about. He made my life miserable. I thought I got rid of him once, but apparently, he just hid better, because I found him again recently. He is just icky. Think slimy, tarry, black ick.

The girl in the corner has been there for a long time. She seems so sad. I can see the shadow of bars across the floor as she sits there with her knees pulled up to her chest, waiting for someone to save her. To set her free. I visited her one day, and she asked me if we were going to leave now. I realized I didn't know how. And that made me sad. But then this girl who has been waiting there for a long time did the most amazing thing—as I sat there absolutely devastated that I did not know how to help her, she sat down beside me and told me it was okay. That we would just wait together, then.

The little girl standing against the wall is just plain angry. She's around three years old, and she is mad. She has been told to stay there, so she does. But she sure doesn't like it. Every time she tries to leave, though, someone puts her back again. I have seen her before and knew she was there. I really saw her in July, when she started yelling at the top of her lungs. Very, very, angry.

The one hidden at the edge of everything is fairly new. Someone who stays in the shadows because she is ashamed to be seen. She's covered in labels that have been thrown at her or given to her over the course of a lifetime, sometimes carelessly and sometimes deliberately. Labels that have stuck:

'mean, 'ugly,' 'fat,' 'uncaring,' 'thoughtless,' 'stupid,' 'lazy,' 'dumb,' 'incapable,' 'slow,' 'unsociable,' 'loner,' 'loser.' She showed some of them to me briefly with that shrug of defeat I feel so often that says, 'Look at me...nobody wants this...nobody wants to see this...nothing will ever make this better...so I just stay here and try not to be noticed...' She wears all of these labels and hides because of them. What she says and what I hear is simply a reflection of what she has come to believe as she has been hiding in the shadows at the edge of whatever is going on. She's there, but she's never a part. She watches intently from the sidelines, but she never participates. Always hidden from view.

It surprised me to see her there.

It surprised me more to see a black panther standing silently beside her, more hidden than she was. Visible only because of his brilliant, piercing, intense green eyes.

The voice of wisdom is rare. I see her clearly in my mind but cannot possibly describe her other than she is a goddess. And when she speaks, I listen.

So there are all of these bits and pieces and things inside. And I have been trying to get rid of them and all of the things I don't like about them (except the voice of wisdom).

Only, here is the thing: these are me. They are a part of me. To try and get rid of them...well, that is just fighting with myself. They are there for a reason. A dear friend once said to me that perhaps all that I needed was a change of perspective. She was right. Two other dear friends recently helped me reframe things in a way that feels so much better.

Let me tell you about all of the awesome parts of me that I am beginning to perhaps see for what they really are.

The gremlin. He doesn't hoard what is ugly and black and bad—he carefully collects those things that have been carelessly tossed aside but that are so essential. Carefully guards and protects those things. Patiently waits. He is watchful and observant and wise in what he picks up. He keeps things safe and is protective and quick to guard. One day soon, I will go and really look at what he is holding on to and treating as treasure.

The imp. He is simply there to remind me of the power of play. Of fun. He reminds me to not take things so seriously, to remember to laugh. Often. Even at myself! Perhaps especially at myself. And to not worry about what others think.

The dragon. He is powerful and free and has incredibly clear long-range vision. He has the power to cleanse and purge what is no longer needed. He is swift and decisive in action.

The cheerleader. She's a peacemaker, not a peacekeeper. She doesn't keep someone else's rules of peace, but she has the power to encourage, to cheer on. To help make peace within and without.

The girl huddled in the corner. She is deeply connected with herself and God. She's in a dream state, an in-between state of clarity and understanding. That huddled position is not one of defeat, but rather where she goes to connect with herself and God. She has powerful clarity.

The little girl against the wall. She listens. She is a very good listener. That is why she is there to begin with: she listened.

The girl in the shadows. She sees everything. She watches and is a keen observer. Without judgment.

The voice of wisdom. Her, I want to keep exactly as she is. I only wish she would appear more often.

Like I said, it's a party inside.

The fun thing is that as I see these things differently, I see myself differently. As I accept more that they have a reason to be there and even begin to embrace them, I accept and embrace me more. All of me. With the characteristics and traits of all of those things. All of them. Me. What I have labeled as 'good' and what I have labeled as 'bad' are really just parts of me. They're always there.

But perhaps they don't all show up at the same time.

A teasing, watchful, fire-breathing angry being who acts decisively and without warning could be a bit overwhelming..."

Can you hear the stories I was telling myself? Can you see the beliefs?

I can. And it astounds me to see how I once treated myself. All else aside, no wonder I hurt so badly! I was tormenting myself.

I don't always remember to be gentle or compassionate with myself. I don't always remember to examine and question what I am thinking. I don't always remember to slow down and quiet my mind and feel for the deeper truths inside.

But when I do, I find the me I have been waiting for.

Who am I, really? I suspect I have just tapped the surface in understanding something that a part of me has known all along.

I am me. And that is all I can be. All I need to be. I am the author of my story.

Part 5: How Good Can it Get?

16

Movement is Life

There is much to be said for doing things that are outside of your comfort zone. Doing things that are new and unfamiliar. In ways you haven't considered before.

My personal belief is that venturing out of our comfort zone is a necessary part of healing and growth—it's kind of like the caterpillar that one day crawls into a cocoon and begins the process of transforming into a butterfly. That can't be a comfortable process! Essentially, the caterpillar digests itself, becoming a caterpillar soup of cells that then rapidly begin to form the features of a butterfly or moth.

Really, that can't be comfortable.

And while metamorphosis is different from what might be considered the healing process, in many respects, it is similar: same cells, different being.

For the last several years, I have felt like my insides have been liquefied. And while the basics of me are still the same, everything else seems to have changed—where I was once a caterpillar, I am now finding out what life is like as a butterfly.

And just like the caterpillar, I am finding that the butterfly also has growing pains. How good it can get is turning out to be a matter of how well I navigate those growing pains and how much growing I continue to do.

As I healed mentally, emotionally, and physically, I mentioned earlier that eventually, I found that I was afraid to move. It's one thing to talk about not hurting anymore, to talk about recovery from chronic pain in the sense that you can move and not hurt: you can stand, walk, and get up and down and *not* feel that constant burning, nagging tightness. It's quite another thing to talk about getting back to doing activities, what we'd call getting back to the life we had. Because you see, there's this part of your brain that's now afraid. Part of you doesn't know how to trust movement.

I found that I didn't hurt. It's been a very long time since I hurt to the degree I did when my life fell apart or when I was diagnosed with fibromyalgia. But just not hurting is not enough—I wanted to move! Only when I started to add activities did I hurt again. And that hurting brought up fear. I was very familiar with the interplay of continued activity causing constant muscle tension that had contributed to my initial spiral downward. Any activity that caused pain to return would kick my brain into high gear, flashing warning signs and lights and setting off klaxons yelling "Danger! Danger!" For a long time, pretty much any activity at all was painful. That scared me.

It requires muscle tension to be active, and it was that muscle tension that got me in trouble in the first place. The pushing through things; the wanting to get stronger. Michael once commented to me (actually, he probably told me many times) that I don't trust myself. He was right. I *didn't* trust myself to know the difference between danger and pushing too hard and the aches and pains that would naturally come as I rebuilt strength and function. No, I didn't trust that I knew the difference, not at all. I kept getting caught in a cycle of increasing my activity—perhaps feeling good moving, perhaps not—and then feeling achy and sore and tight, reminded of how I used to feel. I would have difficulty challenging the belief that I was headed that way again.

Plenty of people will tell you movement is needed to recover from a frozen shoulder or a knee replacement or an injured hip or back or wrist. You might be given range-of-motion exercises or strengthening exercises, but above all, you will be encouraged to keep moving. Intellectually, I know this. But that didn't stop my brain from yelling at me, "That's not the same as fibromyalgia! What about when *everything* hurts?! What about when it hurts worse and doesn't get better?! When it just keeps hurting?!" Nobody ever really has any answers to those types of questions—instead, they just tell you to keep moving. Keep moving through the pain, they say, and it will get better. My experience was that it didn't, though. And I didn't know how to fully trust that it would. I was caught in a cycle of trying and hurting and trying and hurting and not moving forward very quickly at all.

Even as I write this, though, I know it is just an excuse. Because the issue is not about where I've been. I can make it about that and keep it about that, sure, and I can stay trapped in fear. Or I can look at just how good I think it can get. I can examine just what I believe is actually possible for my body.

I challenged that belief directly when I went to my first movement workshop with MovNat.

> *January 14, 2019*
>
> *Day 1: Saturday*
>
> *"Getting tired. Feeling tense. Starting to ache. Starting to think about what it means. Starting to stress. Sitting in the sun at lunch and letting the tears fall. Going back that afternoon. More movement. More limitations. More pain. Don't push*

through the pain, they say. What about when you hurt before you ever started? I wonder. I don't ask until the second day.

Only cry once in class. A split squat to pick up a weight. Or just a split squat, really, because I get painfully stuck at the bottom of the movement. Can't pick up the weight. Can't stand back up. Hot tears.

Most movements are high-intensity workouts for me. Quickly get exhausted. Quick to break a sweat. High-intensity work.

I'm exhausted at the end of the day. Very little energy to do anything other than flop on the bed and cry some more. I have to make myself get up to eat something.

More tears.

Day 2: Sunday

I go in anxious. A jittery, scared, tightly held, vibrating energy inside.

We do a warmup. It's too fast. Too much input. My brain can't process the movement quickly enough. I feel dizziness coming on as I am looking from side to side. I slow down. I focus on my breathing.

The tense, vibrating energy inside is growing.

We start the emphasis part of the workout: 5 deadlifts, 3 jumps, 2 scapular pulls (I plan to just hang). Do the routine for 8 to 10 minutes, the instructor says. Do 4 to 5 rounds. It's not a race, he says.

We begin. I move slowly. Deadlift with great care. The second group is done and the third group is starting their deadlifts before I leave the station.

I move to the jumping station. And freeze. 'I can't,' my brain says. I can barely control the energy inside. I'm feeling overwhelmed. Overstimulated. I stand there.

And someone comes to jump beside me. On the floor instead of on the boxes.

It unfreezes me. I jump. I don't count my steps like we've been told to do. Don't be lazy, the instructor says. You are responsible for your own workout, he says. Count your steps, he says, so you know where you start. And increase each time.

I'm barely listening to him anymore.

I feel like my heart is going to thump out of my chest. I slowly walk to the next station, vaguely aware of people jumping up and grabbing the bar and hanging. It looks so effortless.

The only sound I hear is the pounding of my heart. I look at the bar. And can't will my body to lift my arms high enough to grab it. Another instructor asks if I need help. I'm just going to hang, I say. And I stand there. Can't lift my arms.

Would you like me to show you a regression? he asks. I nod. I'm starting to shake. I'm starting to crack. I reach up for the rings he has lowered to my shoulder height. The motion is too much. I hold the rings and shake more. Feel the hot tears come.

Do you need a break? he asks. Take a break, he says. Only I'm frozen there now. Shaking and crying and cracking apart. I'm not a quitter, I manage to tell him through the sobs. He has someone take me out.

And now it's a full-blown panic attack. I'm having trouble breathing. Tightly pulled inward. Sinking down into the floor, against the wall, hugging my knees tightly to my chest. Feeling the effort of trying to catch my breath.

She's talking next to me. Asking questions. Giving advice. Have I tried this...? Or that...? Every time I start to feel calmer, she talks some more. And the tears start again.

The wall is vibrating behind me as the air exchange system kicks on and off. It echoes the quaking I feel inside.

What if we try some meditation? she suggests. Sit back, slow your breathing, she says.

I scoot back a bit more against the wall and let my legs fall flat to the floor...and feel the full-blown panic again. This is not a safe position!

I bring my knees back up to my chest and restart the process of regaining control.

Eventually, I come back in. Settle inside again. Someone else hands me some ginger and turmeric tea. I'm asked if I'm okay, if I know what's wrong. What triggered it? Did I have breakfast? I hear suggestions about the importance of ancestral healing and listening to my body and feeling vulnerable. I hear 'ketogenic diet' and Brene Brown's name mentioned.

I'm barely listening anymore. Shutting down tightly inside. Closing. 'Don't talk to me like you think I'm beating myself up,' I think. And cry more. In the middle of a meltdown is not the time to try to explain, but I do share a little of my story.

Eventually, I go back in. I watch. Give my brain the activity of focusing on the breakdown of movements I am seeing. Focus there to keep the tears at bay. At least until lunch.

Again, I'm by the wall outside in the sunshine. My sandwich tastes like cardboard. I eat only because I need to. It takes effort. Mostly, I cry.

And go back for the afternoon.

How are you doing? the instructor asks. I'm fine, I tell him. There's really not anything else to say there.

To your credit, he says, from the outside looking in, you look normal.

That doesn't actually help, I respond. And cringe inside.

The afternoon eventually passes. I join a few things. I sit out others. I melt down one more time, that time during a group exercise. We're balancing on a 2x4 and passing objects from one person to the next. I feel my system absorb the weight of the 30-pound bolster and feel a little quaky inside. Feel the impact of the sandbag. Appreciate the respite of small objects.

Now there's one object left to go, and it's the rock. I'm near the end of the chain. By the time the rock gets to me, the room has gone silent. You okay?, he asks. It looks worse than it is, he says. I'm okay.

I feel my body absorb this stress, feel the tension of keeping my balance. Feel the effort of turning... And I can move no farther. The next person has to step toward me to take the rock. A breath passes, and I feel the enormity of what I just did. Meltdown.

And then the workshop is over and I'm on a train headed for the airport and home.

I've cried so much that my eyes hurt. I'm exhausted. Mentally. Emotionally. Physically. I don't really know what just happened. It takes the trip home, a sleepless night, and most of the next morning to start to understand.

I felt threatened this weekend. I had not realized that a part of my subconscious would perceive this workshop as a threat. To everything. To my beliefs about healing. To my plans for certification. To this book I'm writing about healing from chronic pain. But professionally, personally, it was a threat. And somehow, I failed.

And that was overwhelming.

Just tonight a friend defined the following: anxiety = worry and suffering about a future imagined event.

That described me to a tee that weekend.

Only I didn't see that until today.

At one point, I was asked if I had discussed concerns with the instructor prior to the workshop. 'Discuss what?!' I thought. I don't have a medical condition—I have a human condition. That means sometimes I feel overwhelmed and freak out and melt down. It might not happen. But it might. Although if it does, I have no clue what that will look like because it wouldn't really be overwhelming if I did know... 'Discuss what?!' I thought.

I wonder sometimes if I'm reaching for too much, if I should be happy with how far I've come. But there's an internal knowing that says I'm not done, and the knowing is driving me forward. That weekend was a speed bump. A big speed bump. And one I bottomed out on a bit. But ultimately, it's just a bump in the road."

There have been stages and layers of growth in this journey; I've worked through layers of belief about what is possible. I've thrown off what I was told about having to live with pain, thrown off what I was told was possible for my body with regards to work and life, thrown off what I was told with regards to dependence on medication. And now the time has come to throw off believing my own internal chatter about activity.

I went to that first movement workshop with the intent of finding out what it would take to get certified in Level 1 of the MovNat training. Because that is where I am headed next.

I don't need to run half-marathons anymore. I'm no longer running away from things, and I don't need the distraction from my daily life. I actually quite enjoy my daily life.

I want to use movement to heal, not to distract me from the things I don't want to face or be a coping mechanism or a way to prove my worth. I don't want to use movement in a way that numbs me out to how my body is functioning. I don't want to limit movement to linear patterns that ignore the entirety of my body. I want to use movement to recover from my own aches and pains and issues and help others learn how to do the same.

I believe movement is a vital component of healing and something that is often either skipped over or introduced with way too much intensity at the wrong time in the healing process.

That first workshop opened my eyes to just how big the gap is for those attempting to go from recovering from chronic aches and pains to regaining physical fitness and activity.

I intend to help fill that gap. And I am going to do it well.

How do I know I can do this?

Because I have been through the process. I am one of the pioneers. I have recovered from something most people never dream of recovering from. I have found out what it takes by *doing*.

I know because I continue to do it. I'm working with a personal trainer to prepare for the Level 1 MovNat certification later this year. And I *will* certify. If not the first time, then the next. Or the next if need be. I will keep at it until I get it.

I know because of how I feel. And what I can do. I know because things just keep getting better. I work in an amazing clinic that's dedicated to myofascial release and movement. Every week, I get to work with clients who are dealing with pain or limitations in some way. Get to be a part of their process and see their lives change and improve as their understanding of their bodies expands and they begin to heal. I teach a self-care class, and every week, I get to review and practice the principles of softening, exploring, and feeling what is happening in the body and allowing it to change. I get to dive deeply into a healing crisis every now and again as I continue to improve in my own body. Sometimes now I even laugh about it while it is happening.

I continue to move. And feel into how my body responds. I have regained the ability to sense what is going on structurally. That is actually a very big deal. Instead of only feeling painfully stuck in the joints and tissues, I can feel how the stuck areas affect other areas of my body. It's like a light switched on one day and I actually understood physically what I had been trying to wrap my brain around mentally for years: pain is simply a signal that something is stuck. And the stuck something may be far from the area feeling pain. It is that stuck area that I need to feel into.

For years, I've thought that I have a problem with my right shoulder. Until the day I felt how my ribs weren't moving.

And then thought I had a problem with my ribs...

...Until the day I felt how connected my rib issues were to what was happening with the twist and rotation in my pelvis. I've known about the rotation and scar tissue throughout my pelvis for a long time, but I frequently treat other areas that hurt because they are the things drawing my attention.

It is amazing to feel into my body in a different way and recognize just how connected it all really is. And that addressing the structural issues of the pelvis will affect my ribs and shoulder.

How good it can get now is limited only by me. And I intend to keep dreaming big. I keep showing up. I keep feeling.

I did not come this far to not.

17

So What Does This Mean for You?

This could be just be a great (or not-so-great) story about how someone you don't know healed from chronic pain. You may or may not believe what I've shared. That really doesn't matter to me. But if you do believe it and you are one of the many people who are struggling with aches and pains that not only aren't improving but are getting worse, then my question to you is this: what do you believe is possible for your body?

And if what you believe or have been told is that you just have to accept and live with what you are dealing with, do you want to continue believing that?

My journey is unique to me because it is mine, but the messages are everywhere.

For those with eyes to see and ears to hear, messages of hope and possibilities for healing and growth and change are all around us. How lucky I am that I got slowed down enough in my life so that I could see and listen! Slowed down until I heard enough that I could understand.

The messages show up in nature every day in the way that cloudy skies yield to light. The messages show up when rays of sunshine break through and illuminate the edges of some of the stormiest clouds with brilliant light. They show up in the clouds that build out of nowhere and darken the brightest day, when the temperature drops ten degrees in a matter of a few minutes and you know the skies are about to open in a downpour. They come in the shifting of seasons, when the wind blows and the air changes and you know summer is over and winter will be here all too soon. Nature is constantly sending us messages of change and growth.

They show up in the darkness of night that gradually gives way to the rising sun. That one simple act of nature alone gives me reason to hope. I've spent countless sleepless nights waiting for the sun to rise. For some reason, pain always seems worse in the dark and quiet of night, when you're alone and the rest of the world seems to be sound asleep. They're peacefully dreaming, resting their bodies and minds, while you are wide awake, tormented by pain that does not allow you to close your eyes for more than a few moments at a time. I've spent countless nights waiting for the sun to rise, often drifting off to sleep just as it begins to peek over the horizon. Somehow, I'm able to sleep then, because a part of me knows I have survived another night and it is okay to finally rest.

As much as the rising sun has meant hope, there are also messages in the setting of the sun, in the way it gradually gives way again to the dark as night settles in. As much as I've struggled through some nights and don't always like the dark, there is a gentleness to the setting of the sun that speaks to me. Encapsulated in the colors and vibrancy of sunsets is the absolute belief that the sun will rise again.

I've yearned for constancy in my life. Been looking for that place I would one day reach, the place where I would know I have arrived. Where things would no longer change. But that is like asking the earth to stop revolving around the sun. It's not going to happen. I need the dark and the light; I need the periods of resting and wakefulness.

The messages show up in the plants that grow against what should be insurmountable forces of gravity, in seeds buried in the earth that somehow know to push toward light and air, seeds that somehow break free of a hard shell and become a flower or bush or tree. We all have seeds of something inside us. Perhaps they were planted long ago and are just waiting for conditions in which they can have a chance to grow. They don't even have to be optimal conditions—seeds just need a chance for something inside to begin to flower and bloom.

Animals are excellent messengers. I'm fond of turtles and their protective shells, that home they can pick up and move anywhere. The slow, methodical way in which they walk, their gait that can't be hurried unless they are scared. If they really feel threatened, they simply disappear inside. Nobody judges a turtle for doing that. Some of us actually think it is kind of cute; others of us use their drawing-in as an opportunity to pick up the turtle and carry it around. Or we poke at it, trying to get it to come back out.

I have often felt like a turtle: sometimes safe inside my shell, sometimes feeling poked at, sometimes getting moved without my wanting to but being unwilling to come out of my shell to do anything about it. With a soft underbelly of vulnerability that I do my best to never expose. Turtles have great messages for me.

I love butterflies and caterpillars and ugly ducklings, creatures that transform before your eyes in ways that seem impossible and with shapes and colors and beauty that only nature can provide. I love birds and their songs that often go unnoticed, love their playful flight and the way they work together to travel long distances. I love birds that get pushed out of their nests, often before they think they are ready or know that they can fly. But they're nudged to the edge anyway, and then pushed over. I've felt my own wings pinned to my side as I have tumbled painfully to the ground. But I have also felt them spread and open, and as they do, the wind blows in my face and lifts me high into the sky, where I soar for a moment. So many messages that resonate deeply inside, messages about how I have felt in this journey.

Water speaks to me, especially little trickles and streams that find a way wherever they can: over, under, and around obstacles. They have the power to wear away mighty stones and boulders if given enough time. They'll find a way without even trying. They'll join with other small streams and trickles and become rivers and oceans. Individual drops, impossible to count, but that when combined have the power to shape and change our planet. Tides and waves that wash gently—or not so gently—against the shore, inexorably changing it. Sometimes I've felt slammed by a mountain wave of life, tumbling over backwards, coming up briefly for air, only to be slammed again by the next mountain wave. Other times, I've felt the gentle washing of waves over my life, feeling their ebb and flow as they gently pull things out to sea that I no longer need. Beaches are some of my favorite places for learning and listening to the messages nature brings. Where I can so clearly see some of the power and forces beyond our control that shape and mold us.

I've found messages in music and lyrics that have become theme songs and rallying cries inside, words that have spoken to my soul and seem to have been written just for me. Sara Bareilles' "Brave" was the first song I found. I would play it over and over and over on my way to and from appointments. My kids got sick of that song! But I knew how it felt to be stared down by the enemy, to bow down to the mighty. Or to feel the shadow win. For me, there were intense battles happening inside, and her words spoke deeply to that, encouraging me to keep showing up and reminding me I could be brave. Telling me that maybe there was a way out of the cage I was keeping myself in. That *I* was actually the one doing that and that I could let the light in. That things would be okay when I did. Better than okay.

Rachel Platten's "Fight Song" came next, reminding me of "All those things I didn't say, wrecking balls inside my brain..." I didn't know how to take my life back or turn my power on, but I was still fighting. I was too stubborn to give up. I felt like I was losing friends, I often didn't sleep well, and I frequently wondered if I was in too deep. Frequently felt that yes, I was. And I knew people were worried about me. But I couldn't quit, and her words kept speaking to me, showing me there must be a way I just couldn't see yet. Instinctively knowing from the way her words resonated deep inside that there must be more.

I discovered "Dare You To Move" by Switchfoot during my first week of intensive treatment with Michael. "Welcome to the planet," they said. "Welcome to existence. Everyone's here." Everybody was watching me, waiting for me. Truths I could often feel deeply inside. Truths that scared me as they settled in, because what came next would be up to me. "Dare You to Move" challenged me in every way. There were so many times during sessions when I literally felt frozen, stuck, afraid. I felt like I was falling off of the table and hitting the floor, like I was squashed into a corner or against the wall. But nobody was doing that to me; nobody was putting me there but myself. I believed that's where I belonged. I was afraid to move...but then I was nudged along by the words of a song that had been written years before I needed them, words that described that tension I felt so often between who I thought I was and who I thought I could be. Or should be. The song dared me to move, to engage, to show up. The song still speaks deeply to me and has a profound message for those running from themselves: there really is nowhere to go. You cannot escape from yourself no matter how hard you try.

I know. I tried. For a long time.

I found messages in books and podcasts by motivational writers and speakers. More words that resonated deeply inside in a way that felt like they were speaking to me personally, like they knew me personally. It's how I know the lessons must be universal.

For those with eyes to see, the messages show up everywhere. For others, they resonate in a way that perhaps only our subconscious recognizes. It takes repetition before we feel and see the truths there. Marianne Williamson speaks of our greatest fear, and for a long time, I hated that I just knew—in that way many of us just *know* things—

that she was right. I knew that I was afraid of my light. I desperately wanted to find it inside, all the while knowing it was there but afraid of what I thought it would mean. That fight with myself again. Wanting and needing the very thing I was keeping tightly locked down inside.

John C. Maxwell speaks of failing forward; so does Mastin Kipp. Words that resonate even though I often wonder how failure could ever be considered a good thing by anyone. I am aware that perhaps I just need a new definition of "failure," a different perspective on it. I'm still working on that one. But there must be truth in it, because that message keeps showing up.

As do the principles of healing. I believe they are also universal and that healing starts with admitting what we feel. Starts with allowing ourselves to unclench and unbrace and allow ourselves to feel what is there inside. That is when healing can start. Most of us are trying to change how we feel or numb out what we feel. What we need to do is *admit to and allow* what we feel.

I couldn't do that part on my own—I needed help from others who have walked portions of the path ahead of me. John Barnes' myofascial release program has been the means that helped me do that. MovNat is the next step. Allowing myself to get as big as I really am is the goal.

To those of you who feel like your life is headed for a screeching, crashing halt; to those who have already lost the ability to do the things you once loved; to those who refuse to give up searching for a better way to deal with chronic aches and pains, I say this: never give up hope. There is so much *better* than you have been told is possible! Find a myofascial release therapist trained by John Barnes. Register to attend a John Barnes Healing Seminar. Explore how to restore fundamental natural movement to your body. Find those who have walked the path you want to walk and learn from them. Slow down and start to see and listen to what is around you all the time. The messages are there.

There *is* hope. It's not for the faint of heart, and it's not for those who are looking for a quick fix. There is no pill out there that can give you the healing you are looking for. But there *is* hope. There *is* a way. And it is worth every bit of effort it takes to find it!

I am simply another voice sharing the message.

Wishing you all the best on your own journey of healing,

~ *Vanetta*

About the Author

Vanetta's formal education includes an undergraduate degree from Brigham Young University and a Master's degree in Health Promotion from Mississippi State University. She is also a licensed massage therapist and has trained extensively in the John Barnes' Myofascial Release approach. Currently she is working as a therapist and clinic director at the Release Works Myofascial Therapy Clinic in Salt Lake City, Utah. She considers it a privilege to assist others on their journey.

Vanetta loves to travel and explore other places. She now enjoys the active lifestyle she once thought was no longer possible and can frequently be found outside in the sunshine, enjoying time with her family and hiking the trails of Utah, Idaho, and Arizona.

Her travels and continued learning can be followed on her blog at: www.meandmyinnerself.wordpress.com

Notes

Made in the USA
Monee, IL
30 January 2021